D1267048

"Dialog"

Dedicated to my wife, Janet, and to my husband, Roddy.

"Dialog"
What makes a great design partnership.
Ken Carbone & Leslie Smolan

Text by Raul Barreneche

With essays by Massimo Vignelli

and Steven Heller

Pointed Leaf Press, LLC.

www.pointedleafpress.com

"Dialog"
What makes a great design
partnership.

Carbone Smolan Agency
22 West 19th Street, 10th Floor
New York, NY 10011
www.carbonesmolan.com

© 2012 Ken Carbone and Leslie Smolan

All rights reserved under international
copyright conventions. No part of
this book may be reproduced, utilized,
or transmitted in any form or by
any means, electronic or mechanical,
including photocopying, recording,
or by any information storage and
retrieval system, or otherwise, without
permission in writing from the publisher.
Inquiries should be addressed to:

Pointed Leaf Press, LLC.
136 Baxter Street, Suite 1C
New York, NY 10013
www.pointedleafpress.com

Pointed Leaf Press offers special
discounts for our publications, and
signed copies upon request. Please
contact info@pointedleafpress.com
for details.

Company and product names
mentioned herein are the trademarks
or registered trademarks of their
respective owners.

Designed by Res Eichenberger,
Carbone Smolan Agency
Typeset in Kievit
Printed on Hanno Art Bulk 170 gsm

Printed and bound in Italy.

First edition
10 9 8 7 6 5 4 3 2 1

Library of Congress Control Number:
2012942503

ISBN 978-1-938461-02-6

Contents

Foreword

"One of us takes the ball and runs with it, because if we both take the ball, we'll run into each other."

"Our partnership is solidly built on two things: aligned ambitions and trust." Ken

"When it comes to our business, we have dramatically different ways of getting to the same end goal. This kind of creative debate makes for very colorful conversation at times." Leslie

A Design Symbiosis
Massimo Vignelli

Massimo Vignelli is the co-founder of Vignelli Associates, established in 1971 with his wife, Lella. Vignelli Associates is a multi-disciplinary design studio specializing in graphic, interior, product, and furniture design.

One of the most frequent questions Lella, my wife and partner, and I are asked is: "How do you work together?" The answer centers on the basic essence of the nature of collaboration. Working together doesn't mean that you are holding the pencil with two hands, it means that we share the same cultural platform that allows both of us to approach the problem in a way that is complementary, rather than confrontational. This great symbiosis doesn't happen in a day. It starts by sharing a similar approach to every aspect of life and work—from the cultural to the ethical, from the aesthetic to the pragmatic. There is no need to clarify the meaning of words, as the semantics are shared throughout—there are common points of view, and the objectives are clear.

Sometimes there is a difference on how to get there, or how to better express what we want to do. Sometimes one of the two of us may take a certain approach that leads to a wrong turn, and the contribution of the partner consists in pointing out the mistakes and correcting the issue by indicating alternatives or a more appropriate solution to the particular problem. This is one of the blessings of a close partnership, which is based on common respect and trust. When that happens, I do not argue; I know she is right and I toss my drawing in the "round" file. Other times, the contribution happens when one of the partners sees a brilliant approach and the other adds to it, making the end result even better than before. That is a very exciting moment.

There have also been frustrating moments, particularly for Lella, when a macho-oriented business world used to give me more credit, both personally or in publications. For a long time, at the beginning of our career, this happened quite often. At the time, there were fewer women in the profession and men were the ones getting all the credit. It took a long time, the women's liberation movement, and the notion of emancipation, to correct that situation. I remember looking in the mail to check to see if the credits in a magazine article were correct. If not, I would throw away the issue. I did not want to add wood to the fire.

Eventually, the world caught up with us, and our partnership was finally acknowledged, gradually becoming a sort of a brand in itself.

The same is true with my friends Ken Carbone and Leslie Smolan. By now they are a brand, and I love that it makes them one entity in the eyes of the world. No one needs to know where an idea came from, who had the initial sparkle, who took it over, or whose is whose. That is the essence of a partnership. And that is why Design is not Art. Art is usually done by one person. Design can be done by a partnership because it is more of a collective effort than the act of an individual. This doesn't prevent the individuals from expressing and cultivating their own languages. On the contrary. The more they can refine their own languages, the more they can contribute to the evolution of the partnership.

"Dialog" is an active demonstration of a truly successful partnership. It is hard to distinguish the work of one from the work of the other, and that is precisely the main point of a meaningful collaboration.

Will we see more excellence generated by this brilliant team?

No doubt about it!

Ken is one of the best visual thinkers I know.

He can let go and knows how to delegate.

He's multi-faceted and passionate about many things.

He's fast on his feet.

He's extremely persuasive in tough client situations.

He draws very well.

He's a great presenter and likes performing in front of a crowd.

He wins every damn argument.

He sees the big picture clearly but is clueless about the details.

He doesn't hold grudges.

He's extremely loyal and supportive.

He's always moving forward and change doesn't faze him.

He's very logical, pragmatic, and unemotional about business.

He's not about the money.

He thinks the art part is easy.

Leslie has incredible aptitude for the business of design.

She's powerfully creative with photography.

She's all about the details.

She's embarrassingly complimentary about my abilities.

She's deadly patient, deliberate, and process-oriented.

She negotiates legal contracts with ease.

She understands the art of making money.

She wins every damn argument.

She's a fabulous cook.

She's clearheaded and isn't afraid of complexity.

She has a scary intuition about people and clients.

She's a good listener.

She's a devoted friend.

She understands what people want.

She gives people more than they need.

Ken Carbone

Growing up in a blue-collar family rooted in South Philadelphia, art and music were never topics of dinner conversation. However, I've been obsessed with drawing since childhood, and started studying guitar and playing in rock bands in my early teens. In high school, I begged my mother to switch me from a Catholic to a public school so I could take art classes, and lucky for me, she obliged.

Art and music have always been locked in an emotional battle for my creative expression, but a career in art always felt natural to me. When I began my studies at the Philadelphia College of Art, the die was cast. I was fortunate to have influential mentors like Edna Andrade, Kenneth Hiebert, Steff Geissbuhler, Inge Druckrey, April Greiman, and Keith Godard, who saw qualities in my work that steered me from fine arts to graphic design.

I began my professional career in the New York office of Chermayeff & Geismar Associates. Under the guidance of Ivan Chermayeff and Tom Geismar, I worked on prestigious projects for world-class clients. Their artful, multi-disciplinary approach to designing for corporations and cultural institutions served as a model for the design practice I have with Leslie today. Working with Ivan and Tom was an exciting experience that, fortunately, delivered a decisive blow to my aspirations for musical "stardom." Design was now clearly the main course, while guitar playing had become the dessert.

Shortly after leaving C&G, I was recruited by Gottschalk + Ash International, the Canadian firm, to work on design quality control for the 1976 Summer Olympics in Montreal. Fritz Gottschalk, a quintessen-tial Swiss designer, further honed my design skills, and also trained me as a manager. After the Olympics, my visa had expired and I planned to return to the U.S., when Gottschalk proposed I open an office for G+A International in New York City. With no clients and a modest investment, I set up a small office in midtown Manhattan. Slowly, the work came and the practice began to grow. I had just turned 25.

In June of 1977, Leslie joined me as a senior designer, and together we began to attract small projects for museums and corporations. As the business grew, we were made equity partners in the New York office and eventually purchased the business through a leveraged buyout in 1980. This led to the decision to change the name of the company to reflect our ownership, and, as they say, the rest is history.

Now, 40 years after graduation, I still feel that design is the ideal profession for me. It has allowed me to travel the world and work on exciting projects for some great clients. As a child, I could never have imagined that I'd be working in places as far-ranging as Jakarta, Paris, and Kyoto, and creating work that would be recognized worldwide. Design has placed me in an enviable orbit around contemporary life that enables me to experience its many dimensions. It's all of the extraordinary and inspirational experiences I've had—both large and small—that feed my voracious appetite for learning. A career in design presents exciting challenges, both creatively and intellectually, every day.

However, the day this is no longer true, it will be back to rock 'n' roll for me.

Leslie Smolan

People often wonder how I ended up in such a visual family—my older brother Rick is a photographer and publisher, my younger brother, Sandy, a film and television director. The answer is, I really don't know. I was born in 1952 in New York City and grew up in New Jersey, where my father worked as the head of marketing for a pharmaceutical company, and my mother worked part-time as a children's librarian. We were the epitome of the baby boom generation. My parents considered themselves "progressive," embracing modern furniture, the art of Bernard Buffet, and travel to faraway lands.

My mother exposed us to every possible extracurricular activity, and after ballet and art classes, I chose to play the oboe. I joined the New Jersey Symphony Preparatory Orchestra and during summers attended Interlochen, the national music camp in Michigan. In 1970, I attended Indiana University because of their strong music program. I quickly discovered, however, that most musicians were natural performers, whereas I suffered from terrible stage fright.

On a whim, I took an elective course in graphic design taught by a graduate student named Dan Boyarski, who subsequently became a major force at Carnegie Mellon University. I was amazed to find that design satisfied my love of content and desire for personal expression. Once committed to a career in design, I transferred to the Philadelphia College of Art, now the University of the Arts, where the design program was one of the first offshoots of the School of Design (Kunstgewerbeschule) in Basel, Switzerland. It was run by Kenneth Hiebert, a brilliant educator. Despite somewhat makeshift facilities—the building was once an insane asylum—the caliber and quality of the teaching staff was incredible. Steff Geissbuhler, Inge Druckrey, Hans Allemann, Chris Zelinsky, April Greiman, Keith Godard, and Laurence Bach brought the rigor of the Swiss curriculum to America, and began to influence a generation of designers.

My first job was in New York City at a firm that designed annual reports. A year later, I returned to Philadelphia to co-teach a typography class with Hiebert. In addition, I began my own freelance design business and a stock photography agency, handling my brother Rick's images. This more than paid the rent. My entrepreneurial tendencies were already in high gear.

Ken Carbone and I didn't actually meet at school. He'd graduated from the Philadelphia College of Art the year before I arrived, but we moved in the same circles. One day, Keith Godard called to say he'd referred me to Ken, who had just opened the New York City office of Gottschalk + Ash International. Ken offered me the chance to be my own boss and join him in running the studio, an amazing opportunity for a 25 year old.

Over the past 35 years, Ken and I have pursued our interests and passions through the work we do. I often describe a career in design akin to being a perpetual graduate student, as I'm always learning something new and getting a sneak peek into the future.

On the personal front, our lives have stayed in sync as well. Ken married a former client of mine and has three fantastic children. In 1990, I married the amazingly smart, talented, and witty photographer, Rodney Smith. Our daughter Savannah has managed to get a full dose of aesthetics vicariously, yet so far has chosen to be an academic, far from the world of design. Ken and I remain friends and healthy competitors who are egged-on—and delighted—by each other's achievements.

"I take a design problem and carry it around with me, taking my time to decide on the right approach. It's a bit like baking a cake: I make sure I've added the best ingredients before popping an idea into the oven." Leslie

"The French word 'flâneur' refers to someone who strolls around aimlessly, observing and recording the subtle wonders of the world. That's me! A dappled shadow, a rusted door knocker, or a full brushstroke on a masterpiece can inspire an idea. Wandering and wondering is great, but it makes me an awful driver." Ken

Two Heads Are Better Than None

Raul Barreneche

Raul Barreneche, a New York-based architectural designer and journalist, is the author of eight books on architecture and design, most recently *The Tropical Modern House*, published by Rizzoli. He is currently a contributing editor to *Travel + Leisure* and *Interior Design*, and has written extensively for publications such as *Architectural Digest*, *ELLE Décor*, *Departures*, *Town & Country*, and the *New York Times*.

You know the work of the Carbone Smolan Agency, even if you think you don't. If you've ever navigated the labyrinthine corridors of the Musée du Louvre, thumbed through the iconic book series *A Day in the Life*, or wandered through Times Square in the glow of a bright blue sign trumpeting Morgan Stanley's headquarters, you've experienced Ken Carbone and Leslie Smolan's impeccably refined sensibilities. Their visual style is not easily identifiable, mostly because the work looks and feels so perfectly attuned to its context that the design seems to spring from within. Ken and Leslie dig deep to get to the essence of the client and the task at hand, whether it's refreshing an outdated corporate identity or creating a gem of a coffee table book. They uncover the story that needs to be told and communicate it in an eloquent, visual language. "It's never just about surface. There's always a smart idea behind our work," suggests Leslie. "We try to balance style and substance in our approach to design. It's like that classic expression, 'Do we sell the sizzle or the steak?'" offers Ken. "Our projects demand substance. We provide the 'sizzle' to draw people in, but we also deliver a great 'steak.'"

For 35 years, Ken and Leslie have successfully told the stories of huge investment banks and tiny not-for-profits, of world-famous museums and start-up fashion lines, on the printed page, architecturally in three dimensions, and on the digital screen. Now it's time to share the story of their creative partnership. Their lasting collaboration has paired them with an incredibly diverse range of industries, from educational publishers and mutual fund companies to, more recently, white-shoe law firms, restaurateurs, and luxury hotel developers around the world.

Ken and Leslie, one of the design profession's few unmarried male-female partnerships, believe that the key to any successful creative enterprise is a healthy dialog between its partners. And that is how they have chosen to share their story on these pages: as a lively exchange, in their own words, about what has made, and continues to make, their partnership function so well, how they approach the business and art of design, and how their distinct visual lenses shape their work. The four main alliterative chapter titles, "Fame," "Fortune," "Fun," and "Freedom," sum up Ken and Leslie's inspirations for being in the design business—and hint at the creative wit underlying everything they do. The 35 projects featured on these pages are just a tiny sampling of the thousands Carbone Smolan has undertaken in the past three-and-a-half decades.

Ken and Leslie's story begins in 1976, when Ken arrived in New York City to open a satellite office of Gottschalk + Ash International, the design firm where he'd been working in Montreal. Leslie, referred to Ken by a former professor, joined him the following year. The early work was a mix of projects for city agencies and non-profits, like the Flatbush Avenue Development Corporation and the Public Art Fund—projects where a client was willing to give a small firm like theirs a shot, including even a corporate giant like

1976
Public Art Fund
Our very first project was a walking tour guide to public art in lower Manhattan, designed for the Fund's director, Doris Freedman.

1978
Our first employee
Lisa Bales joined our team, and then we were three.

1979
Flatbush Avenue Development Corporation
A 30-foot-tall sculpture marked the frontier of our "streetscape" project for a commercial section of Brooklyn.

1979
Equitable Insurance
This boldly graphic brochure marketed the insurance company's international services.

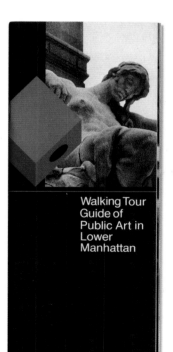

Walking Tour Guide of Public Art in Lower Manhattan

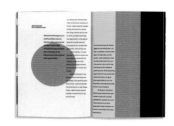

1980
Smithsonian Cooper-Hewitt,
National Design Museum
Our catalog design for an exhibition
about "Tsuba" captured the art
and history of Japanese sword guards.

1981
142 East 30th Street
Our second office was in a carriage
house with a double-height,
sky-lit ceiling.

Citicorp; and big projects with small budgets, like the identity and communications program they created for the American Stock Exchange. Heading up a design firm at such relatively young ages meant a lot of trial and error, a lot of learning by doing. "We had no mentors for this business. We had to learn it ourselves," explains Ken. "We had worked for other people but not in a capacity where we were privy to running the business. We had to do it from the ground up," he suggests. "We made mistakes along the way, but luckily nothing fatal," adds Leslie. "We had the great fortune, very early in our careers, of learning on the job—being put in very demanding situations that made us rise to the occasion. We were educated as designers, not as businesspeople, salespeople, or diplomats," notes Ken.

Mastering those skills helped lay the groundwork for a design firm entirely of their own making, unique in its structure, flexibility, and diversity. "We've tried to be as inventive with the business as we have with the work," explains Leslie. "In many ways, we've designed ourselves." She and Ken have never specialized in any single field or limited themselves to working with specific industries. Nor have they developed a signature design style that clients—or consumers—easily recognize and call on them for. That has made it perhaps harder to categorize their work, but has also allowed them to be nimble and quick on their feet. "We are very curious. We love new opportunities and challenges, so we never specialized, though for a while we achieved critical mass in multiple industries, like educational publishing and architectural graphics for

1983

American Stock Exchange

We developed the identity and communications program for one of the three major stock exchanges.

1984

Museum of Modern Art, New York

Our banner designs, which were part of a comprehensive interior and exterior signage system, welcomed visitors to the museum.

1985

Carbone Smolan Associates

We celebrated the official launch of Carbone and Smolan in the sculpture garden of the Museum of Modern Art.

1985

A Day in the Life

Our book design highlighted the work of 100 photographers who each took pictures in one country on a single day.

AMEX

museums. Those two things are so disparate that people had a hard time figuring out what we did. But we liked it," Leslie admits.

There's been an economic advantage to such creative freedom. "Our business has grown very gracefully and organically over the years. And because of our eclectic interests, we've been able to survive economic ups and downs," suggests Ken. "Having parallel specialties was a sales advantage, too. While we built up expertise in financial services, clients such as Morgan Stanley appreciated that we had a bigger worldview by working for brands like Houghton Mifflin and Christie's, too," he says. "The cross-pollination that we've been able to achieve has kept things more interesting for us as well as for our clients."

The dual engines behind this thriving creative business are the two distinct personalities of Ken and Leslie. Both are extremely creative, energetic, and intelligent—but beyond that, complete and total opposites. "We're equal in willpower and have the same end goal—to do great work in every area of design—but we approach any given problem from opposite perspectives," explains Leslie. "Ken can be extemporaneous and shoot from the hip. I can't do that. I have to dig down and do lots of research to understand what I'm talking about." Ken agrees: "I tend to be fast and nimble, and Leslie tends to be deep and thorough. We are both tenacious, although we have different ways of going about it. I'm strong out of the gate, but Leslie gets us to the finish line." Both partners have strong ideas but distinct ways of communicating them. Leslie's tend to be strategic and editorial; Ken's are more visual. "I start with words and move to pictures," explains Leslie. "Ken starts with pictures and then moves to

1990
AIGA
Our poster for the Communication Graphics Show used reverse psychology to encourage entries for their annual competition.

1991
Macmillan/McGraw-Hill
Spotlight on Literature was a massive undertaking, as we designed and art-directed 28 elementary school textbooks.

words. I'm always thinking, 'What's the concept, what's the message,' whereas he's thinking, 'What will make a strong visual,' and then he'll put words to it."

And there are aesthetic differences to the partners' work. "Ken likes clean, bold, and simple. I like softer, more layered things. Ken's always trying to get to the simplest expression of something, whereas I'm looking for more nuance to the work," says Leslie.

Each of the partners views design through a unique lens, and that leads to the distinct graphic sensibilities that work together under the Carbone Smolan umbrella. Leslie's lifelong passion is photography—right out of college, she ran a stock photography agency for her brother, a noted photojournalist, and she later married photographer Rodney Smith—so she tends to approach graphic design with a photographic eye. As Leslie explains, "I create by collaborating with other artists, always thinking about which photographer or illustrator's style resonates emotionally with the idea. Ken is a true artist—I say he was born with a crayon in his hand. Because of his drawing ability, he can quickly communicate his ideas to clients and designers, and likes to take on the illustration work himself." Ken is forever sketching and painting, as evidenced by his lifetime's worth of beautiful journals. On his desk is a little easel on which he watercolors daily; once a month he organizes life-drawing classes in the studio, where he and fellow artists and designers sketch to the music of Mozart or Thelonious Monk.

Combined, the duo's individual approaches make a formidable artistic force, as Ken is quick to point out. "Leslie is every bit as creative as I am; she just uses

1992
Serenade to a Mac
Ken took a short musical break on his 1933 National Duolian steel guitar.

1994

Baseball: A Film by Ken Burns

We created the off-screen branding, product design, and licensing program to accompany this PBS television series.

1998

Fox River Paper

Our paper promotion showcased the use of illustration, such as the work of Philip Burke, on a range of premium papers.

1998

American Craft Museum

The fundraising promotion for the museum's New York expansion featured foam bricks as the brochure cover.

1999

Dalai Lama

Our poster announced the Dalai Lama's visit to New York and his appearance in Central Park.

1999

Sesame Workshop

We developed the design and branding program for the non-profit children's educational media group.

different tools. Her great talent is in art direction," he explains. "Plus, she's an expert at production, which is essential. I don't have the patience for the details, but Leslie turns the execution of a project into an art itself." Another tool Leslie discovered early in her career was her feminine intuition—a true advantage for a female designer in a then-predominantly male profession. "One of a woman's greatest assets is the ability to trust her instincts. Mine have helped me tremendously during my time in this business, from making decisions on colors, to choosing clients, projects, and staff," avers Leslie.

Framed above a doorway in their office leading to the copy room is a small placard that reads, "The road to success is always under construction." It's a saying that Ken found inside a fortune cookie—and he institutionalized the motto as one of the firm's mantras. "We live by that saying," explains Ken. "We're always tinkering with the business. It has to be agile enough to ride out social, cultural, and economic changes, and we've been through so many in 35 years." Indeed, he and Leslie have not only adapted and survived the challenges of three-and-a-half decades, but they continue to do highly visible, award-winning work, in great measure because of the lively and productive dialog between the partners. The projects on the following pages offer a chance to listen in on their conversation and hear the stories behind such significant work.

1999
The Virtuoso
Authored by Ken, this book featured profiles of living legends in art, music, and culture, with photographic portraits by Howard Schatz.

2002
Carbone Smolan Agency
"No Time to Lose"
We designed a promotional watch as a gift for clients and friends.

2005
Brooklyn Botanic Garden
Our logo design, communications program, and website helped establish this non-profit as a world-class institution.

2012
Office of the Carbone Smolan Agency, New York
This 10,000-square-foot space has been our office for the past 21 years.

"It's never just another project to me: I'm as passionate about our clients' projects as they are, if not more so. And that sincerity is appreciated because people keep coming back to us." Leslie

"I don't have a dream project—I have dream clients. If the rapport with a client is great, rest assured the project will be great." Ken

Playing Favorites
Steven Heller

Steven Heller is the author, co-author, and editor of more than 140 books on design. He was an art director for the *New York Times* for more than 33 years, and is currently co-chair of the MFA Design: Designer as Author + Entrepreneur department at the School of Visual Arts in New York.

A designer's favorite work is an indication of many things. Pride in craft and concept. Joy in problem solving. Elation in the outcome. Of course, sometimes a designer's favorite work is not the most commercially successful. But designers are artists too, and their best designs must be seen and appreciated through their personal lenses.

I asked Ken Carbone and Leslie Smolan to share their faves with me. From 35 years of work, they selected three: Aether Apparel sportswear, the signage system for the Louvre, and Nizuc, a resort and private residences on the Riviera Maya. These three are not atypical clients for a firm as reputable as theirs. The work covers a broad range of companies and institutions that demand and employ good design. But the designs they received were not typical —they were indeed special. Not because they broke uncharted design territory, but because their design components were so elegantly refined.

If I had to define Carbone Smolan's place in the design universe, refinement is the first word in a sentence that would read: Refinement and elegance are the armatures on which all of CSA's projects are produced. Of course, they start with content merged with form. Functionality is essential. But the result is neither trendy nor fashionable. Rather, it is impeccably contemporary and invariably perfect, precise, and refined.

Now, within all that, there is wit, too—when appropriate. But whenever I see CSA's work, I know that after all the forethought and research, the sketching and rendering, the exacting composition of type and image, paper and ink, and everything else that makes quality design, wit is what guides the process.

Fame

He likes the spotlight; she prefers being beh
the scenes. He relishes the pitch; she revels
the work speak for itself. She'd rather show;
rather tell.

As the two halves of the Carbone Smola
Ken Carbone and Leslie Smolan are as famou
graphic designers can be. "Fame in the desig
is a relative term," notes Ken. But their indiv
takes on being in the spotlight are polar op
"Ken's a born performer. He likes being visib
front. I prefer that the work be so powerful
it sells itself, so I don't have to do a lot," say
She's the producer of this fame game, Ken i

"Being associated with famous things—working with the Musée du Louvre or the White House—is fame enough for me," says Ken. "I'd rather be Dieter Rams than Philippe Starck. Philippe Starck is more famous, but Dieter Rams is very, very well respected and has been for a really long time." But he recognizes the benefits of notoriety: "Fame is street cred. It brings recognition, visibility, and respect." Leslie adds: "What fame does is increase awareness that we exist and we do good work." For her, it's always about the work.

Things change, though. "In the beginning, I think working for a famous person or brand was a motivator for Ken. Now we've switched. Designing for big names like Baccarat and Mandarin Oriental is more important to me," says Leslie. "Fame adds to the motivation."

In the end, personalities aside, do they want to be famous?

Leslie: I'm not looking for personal recognition. But I think Ken would like to be famous.
Ken: I want to be remembered. That's different.
Leslie: Would you want to be profiled in *The New Yorker*?
Ken: That would be great. But I'd rather get to design the cover of *The New Yorker*.
Leslie: You'd rather do the cover than have a profile in the magazine?
Ken: Absolutely.
Leslie: Why not both?

Indeed.

Punta Nizuc, Mexico, 2007   Our branding for Nizuc turned an empty stretch of sand into an ultra-luxurious resort. Even without a single building on site, we generated great buzz and put a completely unknown brand—and a young, dynamic developer—on the international stage. Ironically, it has become one of our most famous projects.

Starting with nothing but sand and sea was actually liberating. We did our homework and discovered that Punta Nizuc was identified on ancient Mayan maps, and in English meant "nose of the dog." For elegance and clarity, we shortened the resort name to Nizuc and designed a modern Mayan glyph as the brandmark. The strong iconic symbol lent itself to creating beautiful black-and-white patterns, so we designed and produced objects of desire—from amulets and cookies, to sarongs and flip flops—to make the brand feel tangible and real.

To create the experience of being at Nizuc, we staged an elaborate on-site photo shoot, embedding our branded products into the photography. We cast models to imbue our images with life. We let the pictures speak for themselves and kept the text minimal, immersing potential guests and real estate buyers into the world-class architecture, wildlife preservation, and natural landscape, as well as referencing a level of service that would redefine luxury in Mexico.

A two-volume hardcover coffee table book captured the soul of the destination.

This project just came together on every level. The site was stunning, and we were given free rein to imagine the possibilities. Our passionate client, Alan Becker, was like a kid in a candy store every time he saw new design concepts. We decided to tell the story of a magical place where the spirit of the ancient Mayans inspires the twenty-first century.

"NIZUC WAS DEVELOPED FROM THE HEARTS OF MANY PEOPLE TRYING TO ACHIEVE EXCELLENCE."
Adrian Zecha, Founder, Amanresorts

One-, two- and three-bedroom residences are seamlessly integrated with nature. A warm, subtle palette sets the stage for a dramatic centerpiece: a private infinity pool, from which one can take in the most brilliant views of the sea and sky.

9

Seven 18-hour days of photography created a series of images that celebrated beauty, magic, design, high-end luxury, and otherworldliness. These images were then stitched together like a film, juxtaposing still-life images with landscapes, luxury objects with cultural artifacts, and moments in time with objects from nature.

70

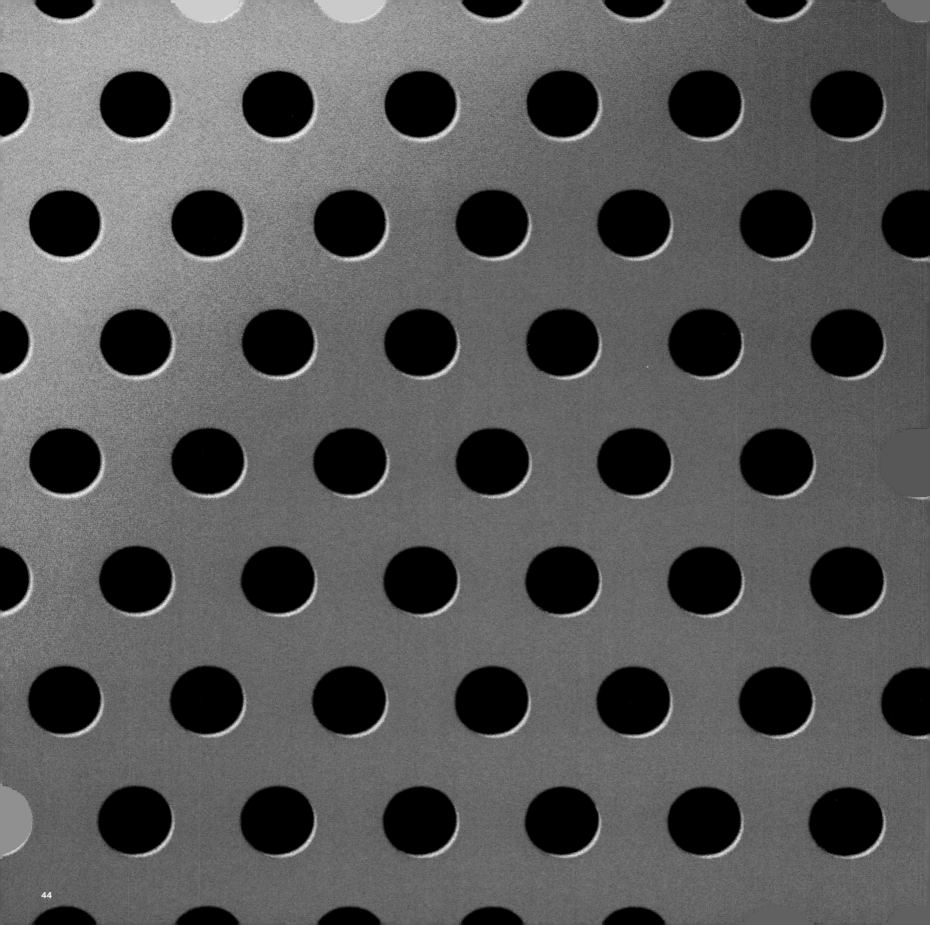

New York, NY, 1980 An instant landmark on the Manhattan skyline, Citicorp Center was a pioneer in adding shops and restaurants to office buildings. The exterior signage we proposed was fought every step of the way by middle managers who protested: "It won't withstand the wind." "It's too big." "It can't be red." A year later, we made a presentation to the chairman of Citicorp. He took one look at our design and approved it on the spot.

This project was like on-the-job training. Most of our signage work up to this point was easy by comparison. Here, we were challenged to design something iconic for a gleaming new corporate tower with a signature triangular crown, smack in the middle of Manhattan. We quickly found a consulting engineer (a tough German named Werner) who looked at our models and told us what would work and what wouldn't, without destroying our design. We learned about wind loads, material stresses, colorfast finishes, and that the word "cantilever" meant something more than a lucky move in Scrabble. We chose to use perforated metal to reduce the overall weight of the sign and painted multiple triangular panels bright red to create impact on the street.

Boston, MA, 1991 Our playful, consumer-friendly system for asset manager <u>Putnam Investments</u> was a complete game-changer. It turned the entire industry on its ear and set a new standard for selling and marketing mutual funds. I still remember Ken asking me after our first meeting with the client, "What's a mutual fund?"

The Putnam Fund for Growth and Income

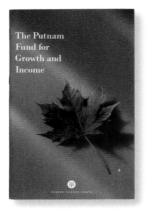

Putnam Utilities Growth and Income Fund

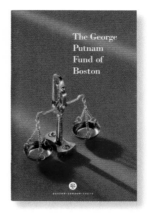

The George Putnam Fund of Boston

Putnam Dividend Growth Fund

Putnam Equity Income Fund

Putnam Convertible Income-Growth Trust

Putnam American Government Income Fund

Putnam Managed Income Trust

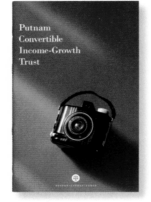

Putnam Minnesota Tax Exempt Income Fund II

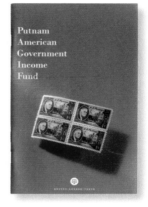

Putnam Tax-Free High Yield Fund

Putnam Municipal Income Fund

Putnam New York Tax Exempt Opportunities Fund

Putnam Texas Tax Exempt Income Fund

Putnam Tax-Free Insured Fund

Putnam Pennsylvania Tax Exempt Income Fund

Putnam Arizona Tax Exempt Income Fund

We first took Putnam's 80-something individual funds and organized them into four simple, color-coded categories of investing. We then photographed small-scale objects, either from nature or antiques, to become the "icon" for each fund. Our intent was to demystify the process of investing for individuals. After our design presentation, the CEO exclaimed, "I hired graphic designers and got management consultants!"

The standard approach for marketing brochures at the time was to show a retired older couple sitting in rocking chairs on their front porch, for example. As Baby Boomers, these images certainly didn't resonate with us—and we were the target market. Sometimes I think ignorance is the most useful skill we have. We got to challenge the norms and it worked.

Putnam
Investors
Fund

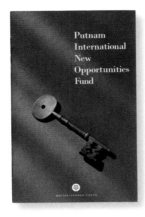

Putnam
International
New
Opportunities
Fund

Putnam
Vista
Fund

Putnam
Global
Growth
Fund

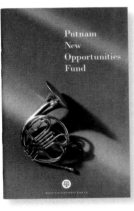

Putnam
New
Opportunities
Fund

Putnam
Health
Sciences
Trust

Putnam
Voyager
Fund

Putnam
Asia Pacific
Growth
Fund

Putnam U.S.
Government
Income Trust

Putnam
Diversified
Income
Trust

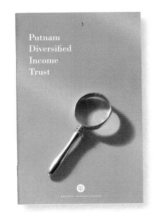

Putnam
High Yield
Trust

Putnam
Income
Fund

Putnam
Adjustable
Rate U.S.
Government
Fund

Putnam
High Yield
Advantage
Fund

Putnam
Global
Governmental
Income Trust

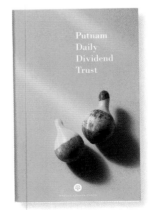

Putnam
Daily
Dividend
Trust

Paris, France, 1988 For the past 25 years, our signage system for the <u>Musée du Louvre</u> has helped more than 150 million visitors find the Mona Lisa, the Venus de Milo—and the *toilettes*. It's now a permanent part of the museum, literally carved into the building's honey-hued limestone walls.

One day, we received a telegram out of the blue asking us to submit our portfolio for a signage project at the Louvre. Thinking it was a prank from some Parisian friends, we ignored it. The telegram turned out to be a legitimate invitation to a coveted international competition—which we eventually won.

When we received the competition requirements, the stack of documents measured a foot high and were all in French. One word came to mind: *Merde*.

```
WESTERN UNION
13022 HOLLENBERG
BRIDGETON MO 63044 19AM
```

Western Union Mailgram®

```
1-016918A353 12/19/85 ICS IPMBDGD BTN NYAA
03161 BRIDGETON MO 12-19 0348P CST BDGC


CARBONE AND SMOLANE ASSN
170 5 AVE
NEW YORK NY 10010



1-013281A353 12/19/85
ICS IPMRYNB RNO
 04271 12-19 1137A PST RYNA
1-106744G353 12/19/85
ICS IPMIIHA IISS
  IISS F M FCH 19 1000
PMS NEWYORK NY
FCA223 FUF714 ZTP257 TTP324
USNX CO FRXX 050
PARIS 50/43 19 1542
TF8070011
CARBONE AND SMOLANE ASS.
170 FIFTH-AV
NEWYORKNY10010
ABOUT SIGNAGE SIGNALETIC AND INFORMATION SYSTEM CONSULTATION
ON THE NEWS-PAPER LE MONDE OF DEC 19TH,85
PLEASE CAN YOU SEND YOUR REFERENCES FOR THE MUSEUM BEFORE JANUARY
6TH,86
                    GRAND LOUVRE MUSEUM
                    2 PLACE-DU-PALAIS-ROYAL
                    75001-PARIS
                    TEL 1-43-26-90-12
NNN
1419 EST

1648 EST


16:54 EST

MGMCOMP
```

5241 (R 7/82)

TO REPLY BY MAILGRAM MESSAGE, SEE REVERSE SIDE FOR WESTERN UNION'S TOLL - FREE PHONE NUMBERS

We had a month to prepare for the presentation to the competition jury in Paris. The pace was intense, and demanded a daily "charrette" of concept sketches. Our final submission was a 100-page book outlining our process and design intent. The museum sent one plane ticket, and Leslie decided I should go alone. At the presentation, which was held in a palatial hall in the Louvre, there was a jury of about 25 competition judges made up of architects, designers, and government officials. There was also a translator who I thought was butchering my presentation. I had a basic knowledge of French, so I asked if I could deliver the rest of the presentation myself. This proved to be a smart move: The jury immediately paid more attention to what I was saying, and at times, even helped me with my pronunciation.

The competition for this project was fierce, with a number of design firms participating that had much more experience than Leslie and I did. Before we received the letter confirming our win, the client called to say "Vous êtes le lauréat!" Working for a foreign government, running a foreign office, designing in a foreign language, and being paid in a foreign currency—the project couldn't have been more challenging. But 36 trips to Paris helped to ease the pain.

The typeface we chose for the project was Granjon, which has French origins and worked well in the wide variety of signage techniques we employed. It looked especially beautiful hand-carved in the limestone walls of the main visitors' reception hall.

ÉTABLISSEMENT PUBLIC DU GRAND LOUVRE

Le Président

Paris, le 3 octobre 1986

Objet : Concours de concepteurs "Signalétique du Grand Louvre"

Monsieur,

J'ai l'honneur et le plaisir de vous informer que, à l'issue des délibérations du jury, et sur proposition de ce dernier, vous avez été désigné lauréat du concours de concepteurs "Signalétique du Grand Louvre".

Conformément à l'article 9 alinéa 2 du Règlement Particulier du Concours, il a été établi, à l'issue d'un vote, le classement suivant :

1. **Carbone Smolan Ass.**
2. Chermayeff & Geismar
3. Total Design
4. Bill Cannan
5. Visuel Design et Laser Image
6. Geriau
7. D.G.W.

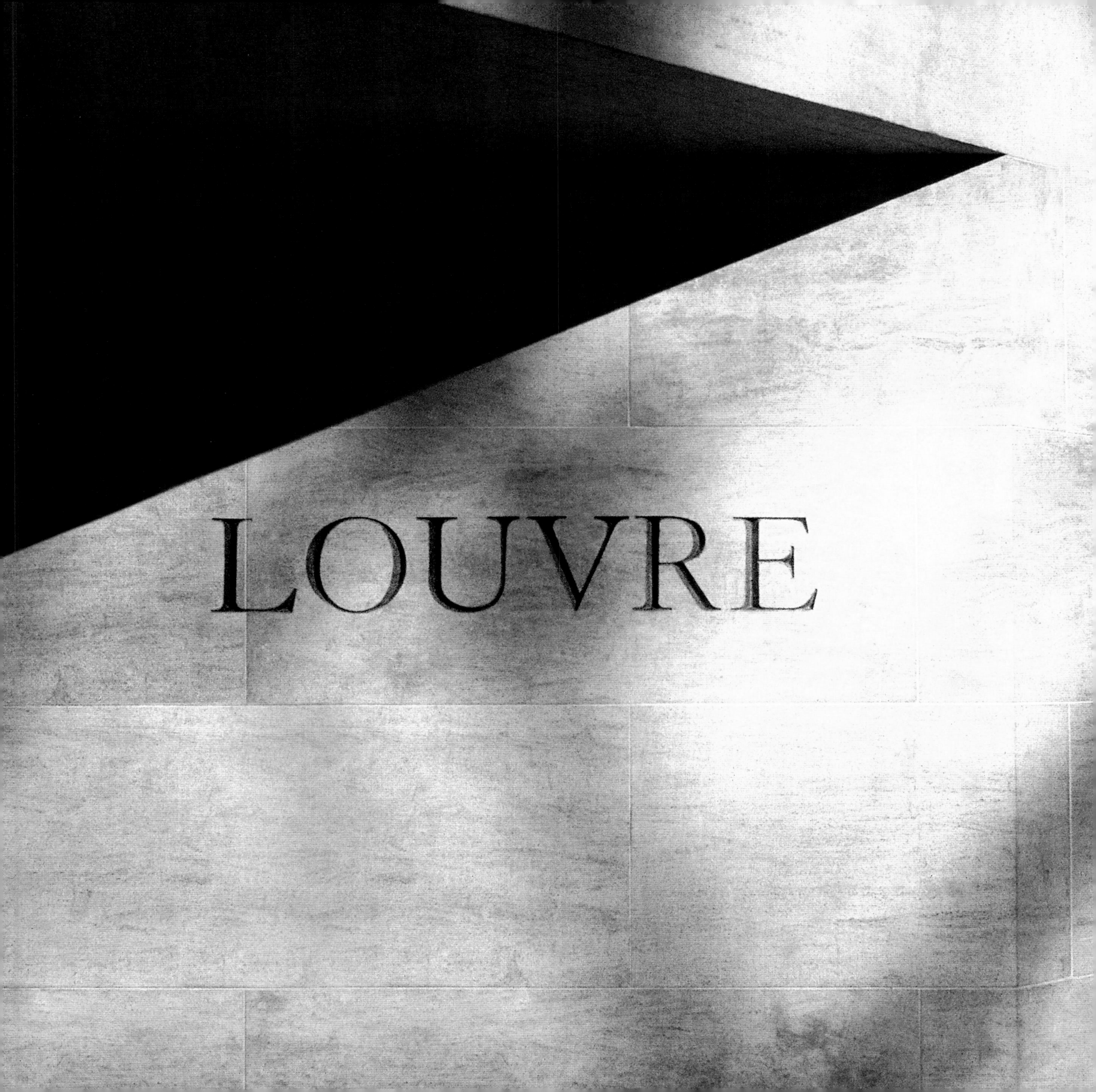
LOUVRE

Working with architect I.M. Pei and his team, we integrated major directional and information signs into the architecture, including one immense wall where we displayed images of the Louvre's "greatest hits." Images of the Mona Lisa and the Winged Victory helped to quickly direct visitors to popular collections. Our signage system mirrored Pei's use of refined materials— glass, stone, and steel—to subtly complement the architecture and the grand spaces while being visible enough to guide the international visitor.

Early in the project, our client gave us a critical choice: The system had to be designed either in five languages or only in French. We decided on just using French, but with a twist. Echoing Paris' own *arrondissement* system, we created a universal numbered plan that, when keyed to handheld paper guides in multiple languages, accommodates the constant relocation of the collections, and guides visitors through the museum.

We scaled the signs appropriately to the given spaces, with larger structures for intersecting points of circulation such as stairwells, and smaller wall-mounted elements in areas near the collections. Someone once asked me how I felt about working on this project, to which I responded, "Pretty great, since I now have more work hanging in the Louvre than any other artist."

New York, NY, 1997   It's always a thrill to design a magazine. But the stakes are higher when you're asked to remake a design-world stalwart like *Architectural Record*. And having to follow in design legend Massimo Vignelli's footsteps—now that *really* makes you sweat.

The logo for *Architectural Record* had to be simple and bold enough to be superimposed on dramatic cover shots. We modified the Bell Gothic font, set it in all caps, and used it in a range of colors to give the logo the strength it needed. Our design for the entire magazine followed a principle of simple typography, strong page layout, and an efficient and flexible format.

ARCHITECTURAL RECORD

ARCHITECTURAL RECORD

ARCHITECTURAL RECORD

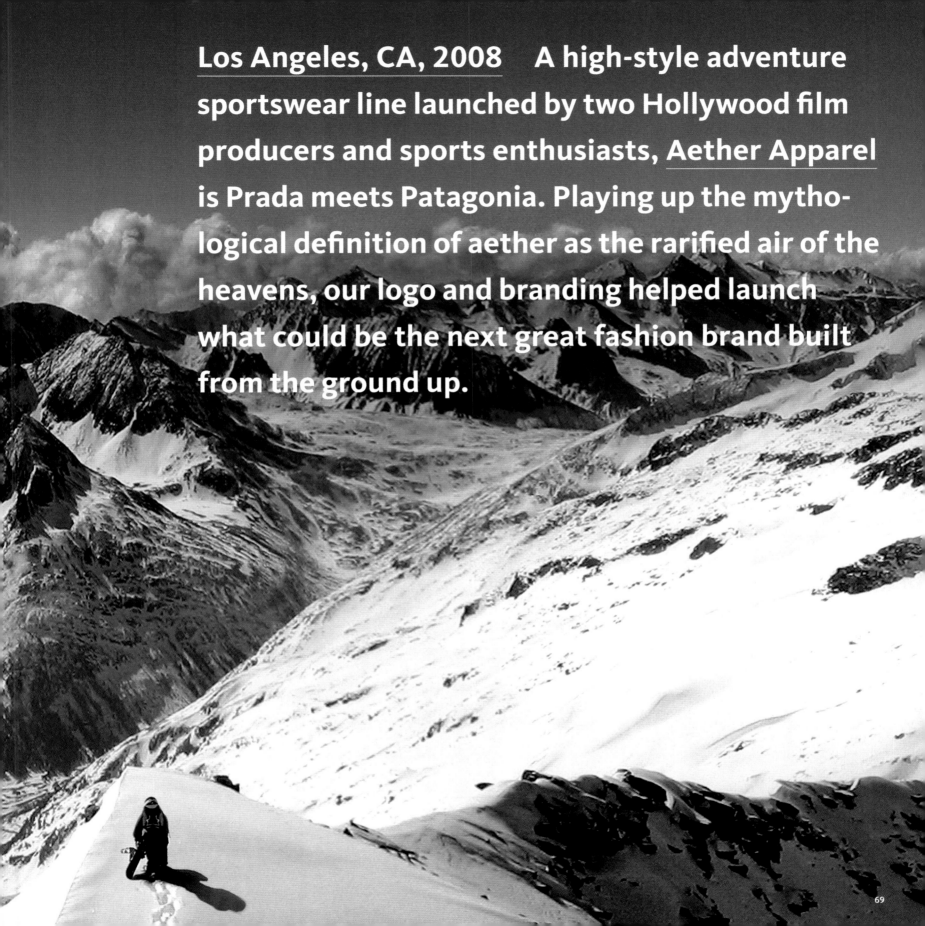

Los Angeles, CA, 2008 **A high-style adventure sportswear line launched by two Hollywood film producers and sports enthusiasts, Aether Apparel is Prada meets Patagonia. Playing up the mythological definition of aether as the rarified air of the heavens, our logo and branding helped launch what could be the next great fashion brand built from the ground up.**

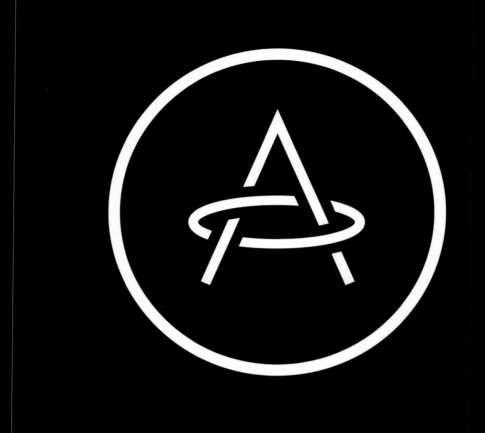

By any measure, this was a brave client. Well in advance of product development, the entrepreneurs, Palmer West and Jonah Smith, focused on building a holistic brand identity for their stylish, high-performance sports apparel.

Our linear "A" symbol, referencing both the clouds that gather at the top of mountain peaks and infinity, became the central element of the branding, and was applied to everything from the website to product accessories such as an S.O.S. whistle that comes with every purchase. In addition, photography featuring the beauty and purity of wilderness destinations (the playgrounds of Aether's customers) complemented images of the clothing.

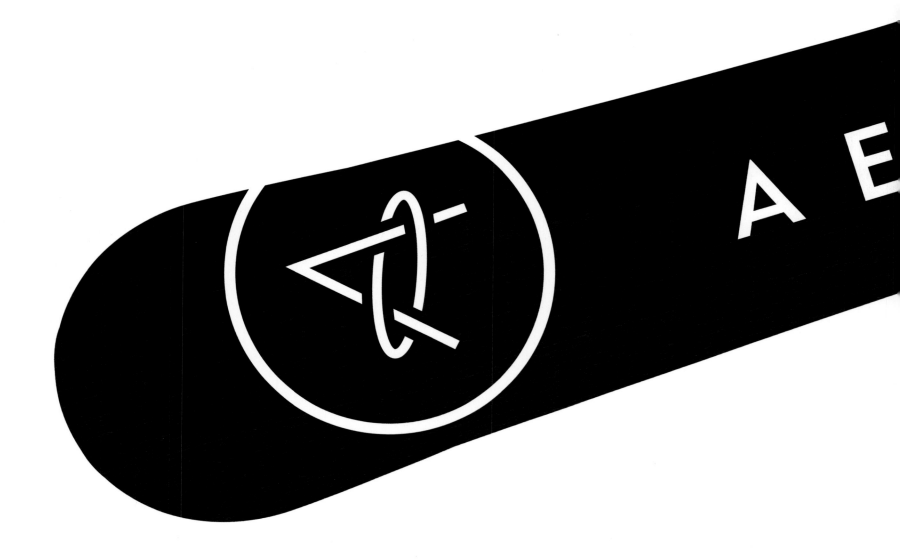

THER

There was a great sense of collaboration throughout the project, with the client suggesting unique promotional ideas, like a branded snowboard. This was very helpful, since neither Leslie nor I are ever on the ski slopes.

As the product began to take shape, our symbol became a subtle accent on labels and catalogs. I particularly appreciated the owners' "soft sell" philosophy about branding. This was in contrast to the current trend of some fashion companies, where an oversized logo on a jacket turns their customer into a walking billboard for the brand. Aether also demonstrates confidence in the quality of their line through the low-key style and modest size of their product catalogs.

FALL 09

AETHER

When it came to photography, we played a supporting role and consulted on general style. West and Smith both have a strong visual aesthetic and we trusted them to create the "Aether look" photographically. We designed the best format and layout to support that imagery in catalogs.

SUMMIT **JACKET** DARK EARTH

DARK EARTH

04

Pairing detailed product photography with dramatic shots of nature, where the color of one image enhances the other, further contributed to the brand identity of this young, distinctive company.

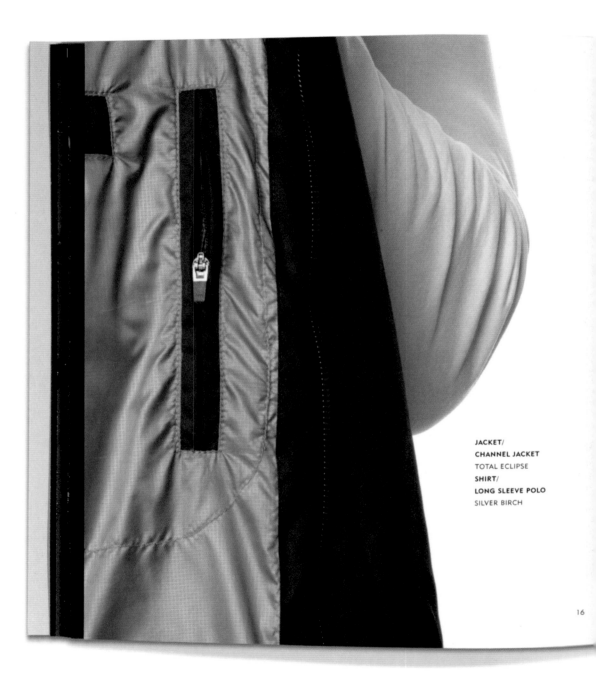

JACKET/
CHANNEL JACKET
TOTAL ECLIPSE
SHIRT/
LONG SLEEVE POLO
SILVER BIRCH

16

ALVAR AALTO
LIVING DESIGN

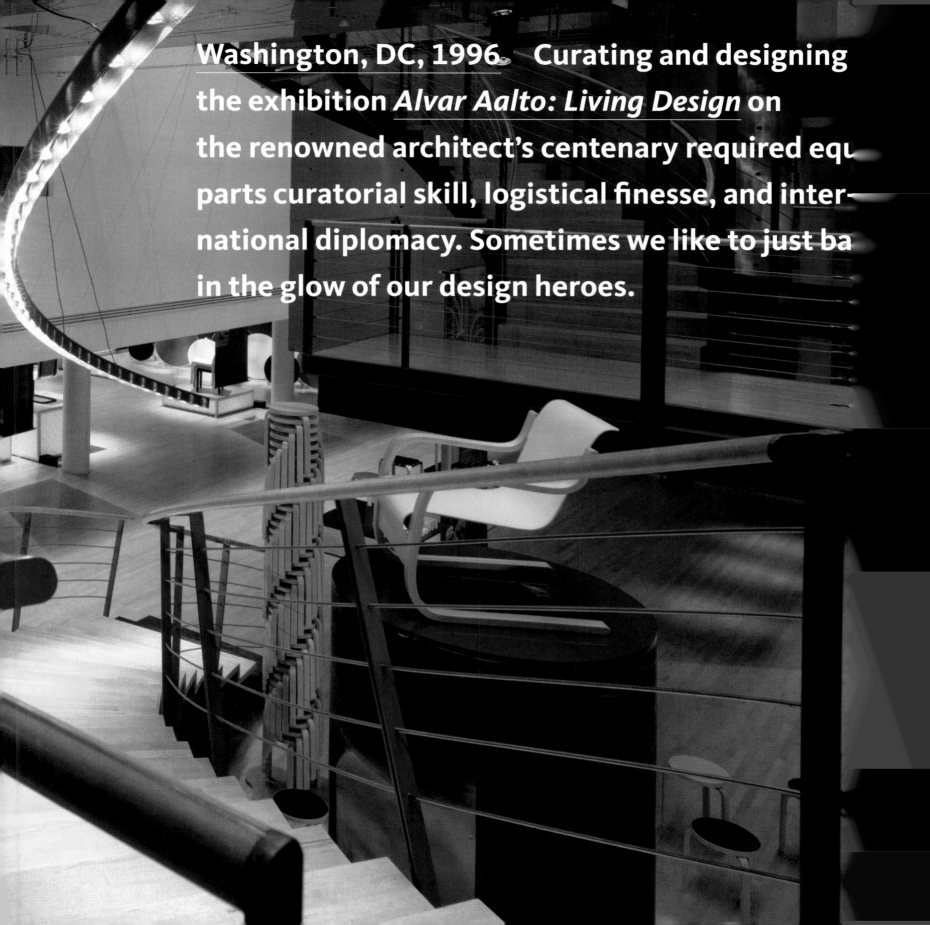

Washington, DC, 1996 Curating and designing the exhibition *Alvar Aalto: Living Design* on the renowned architect's centenary required equal parts curatorial skill, logistical finesse, and inter-national diplomacy. Sometimes we like to just ba in the glow of our design heroes.

EXPERIMEN

A PENCHANT FOR PROCESS

In a famous quote, Aalto called the chair a leg or a table "the little sister of the column." The importance of the column in architecture explains Aalto's dedication to the development of this part of his products.

Finland abounds with birch trees, and her craftsmen have worked with birch since before history. Other innovators of bent wood furniture design in the early part of the century, however, were working primarily with beech and other woods that were available in their countries and whose inherent qualities were appropriate for their designs. Aalto's challenge was to apply the theories of new design from Germany and other countries to the traditional methodologies and most abundant material of his homeland. In fact, Aalto's task was to invent the particular type of furniture for which birch is appropriate. Here the material is truly the progenitor of the form.

PRODUCTIVITY

Aalto saw the industrial assembly line as a social benefit, making studio products available to the greatest number of people. As always, he was able to balance this with an appreciation for hands-on craftmaking. The Aalto system of manufacturing reptile industrial expresses, preferring a synthesis of the benefits of both industry and craft.

MAKING AALTO'S FURNITURE

When we curated the exhibition *Alvar Aalto: Living Design*, we realized that some examples of Aalto's work could be found only in the designer's native Finland. When the Finnish government said certain objects, such as original furniture prototypes, were not allowed to leave their country, we said, "They're not. The Finnish Consulate is Finnish territory in Washington, D.C." So some of the finest examples of the Modernist master's furniture, textiles, and lighting made the trip to Washington.

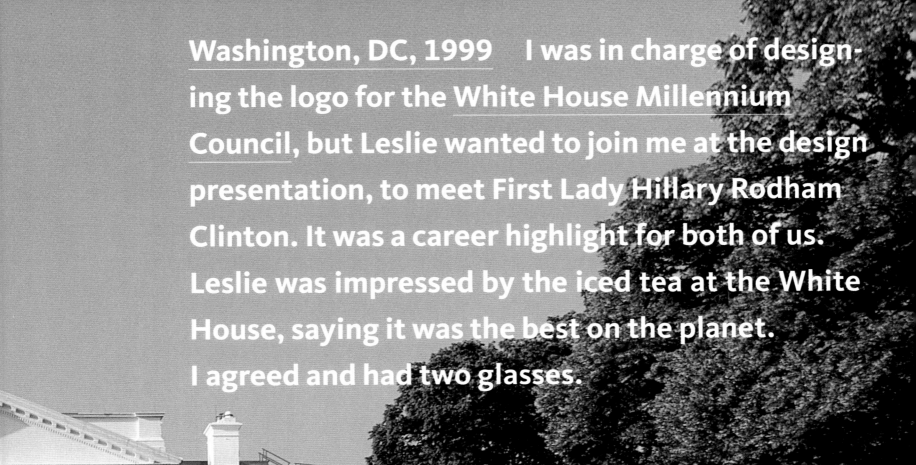

Washington, DC, 1999   I was in charge of designing the logo for the White House Millennium Council, but Leslie wanted to join me at the design presentation, to meet First Lady Hillary Rodham Clinton. It was a career highlight for both of us. Leslie was impressed by the iced tea at the White House, saying it was the best on the planet. I agreed and had two glasses.

The White House Millennium Council was created to celebrate achievements of notable Americans, initiate and highlight local millennial projects, and encourage efforts to preserve America's treasures, such as the original flag that inspired Francis Scott Key to pen the "Star-Spangled Banner." The identity would link diverse projects over three years with the theme "Honor the Past, Imagine the Future."

We presented three designs to the First Lady. She chose the logo, designed in a long, vertical banner-like shape that depicts a path to a future horizon, with three stars representing the next millennium. She suggested that we add red to our proposed monochromatic blue and white design.

In the spirit of democracy, everyone in the studio participated in the design process.

2000

WHITE HOUSE
MILLENNIUM COUNCIL

Fortune

Ken and Leslie recognize their engagement in the delicate balance between art and commerce. As Ken points out, "This is a business, not an artist's atelier." Leslie adds: "A lot of design firms go out of business because they don't know about money. Art is important, but it takes both parts. I'm very focused on making us a healthy, profitable organization." Ken admits: "We are a very well-oiled machine, and that is 100% due to Leslie's know-how. If she wasn't my partner, I would have gone out of business years ago."

This isn't a case of one partner playing artistic director while the other balances the books. Leslie just happens to be blessed with a nose for business as well as an eye for design. There is creative input from both sides, though the scales tip toward Leslie when finances are involved. "Ken and I have arguments about how much to charge people. The joke between us is that I should bid the job and Ken should design it," notes Leslie. "Usually, if I estimate the project and he drives the creative part, that's the sweet spot." Carbone Smolan's work has been both profitable and influential—not an easy achievement.

What does financial success mean to Ken and Leslie? "For me, money is how I keep score," says Leslie. "In a field where measuring success is very difficult, that's one gauge." Major financial clients like Morgan Stanley obviously fit the bill (and pay the bills). But the partners take on plenty of work for not-for-profits, too, including the Natural History Museum of Los Angeles County. "We don't have to make money on every project," offers Ken. "When we make money for the clients, that's often reward enough for us."

Leslie: I grew up in a very business-minded family that always had us working to earn money—babysitting, selling greeting cards door-to-door, waiting tables. Ken grew up very poor. His mother had a hard time putting food on the table. So he grew up with no money at all. When I met him he couldn't even balance a checkbook.

Ken: I still can't.

Leslie: Ken can be totally unaware of his own worth. He always charges too little.

Ken: I remember my mother, a devout Catholic, saying, "Money is the root of all evil." There's something in my genes that resonates with that. Money is just not a thing I like to focus on. I like having money and I like spending money. I dislike making it.

Leslie: In our relationship I look like the big spender but I'm actually pretty conservative.

Ken: But you are the big spender!

Leslie: Only on the work. I always say, if the work is great, no one ever remembers what it cost. But if it's a failure, the clients will always remember it as having been too expensive—no matter how little they actually paid.

Making money really is an art.

New York, NY, 2008   We positioned this sleek, testosterone-fueled sales and marketing campaign for the W New York/Downtown, the hotel group's first residential development in the city, as the ultimate bachelor pad for young, aggressive Wall Street types. They're the kind of apartments that say power, money, and control—perfectly suited to "Masters of the Universe."

All the applications of our design, from a branded bottle of water to the angular-shaped acrylic cover on the sales brochure, were aimed squarely at the young, metrosexual male investment banker in the market for a high-style condominium around the corner from Wall Street. Clearly, these were not apartments for me, and Leslie commented that the design program recalled the feeling of shiny black sports cars.

W

NEW YORK DOWNTOWN

HOTEL & RESIDENCES

16.9 fl. oz. (500mL) Bottled Water

The client brief suggested that the look of all the marketing materials be "techno-glam," meaning very high-tech with a high-fashion edge. The apartments' sexy, non-traditional interiors, with their polished surfaces and sharp angles, were glamorously rendered and featured in our 40-page brochure that described the lifestyle and amenities available to prospective buyers.

City dwellers are always on the go—which means they need a go-to place for relaxation 24/7. Not to worry—W New York Downtown residents have an all-hours amenities floor of their very own. Cloud 9 is good. Floor 31 is even better.

◄ DIGITAL LOUNGE
Our media floor passes even the most competitive screen test—with its large flat screens, video game systems, wireless internet and cushy sofa sitting area.

SHOW
(MEDIA SCREENING ROOM)
Host extraordinary film parties that will make your guests feel like the celebrities they're watching.

CAFE
Satisfy your mind, body, spirit and caffeine cravings in our residents-only cafe.

The high-finish, extreme geometry, and red-and-black branding theme was also applied to complimentary briefcase-style shopping bags. The website combined all of these design elements, complete with animations to draw attention to life at the W New York / Downtown.

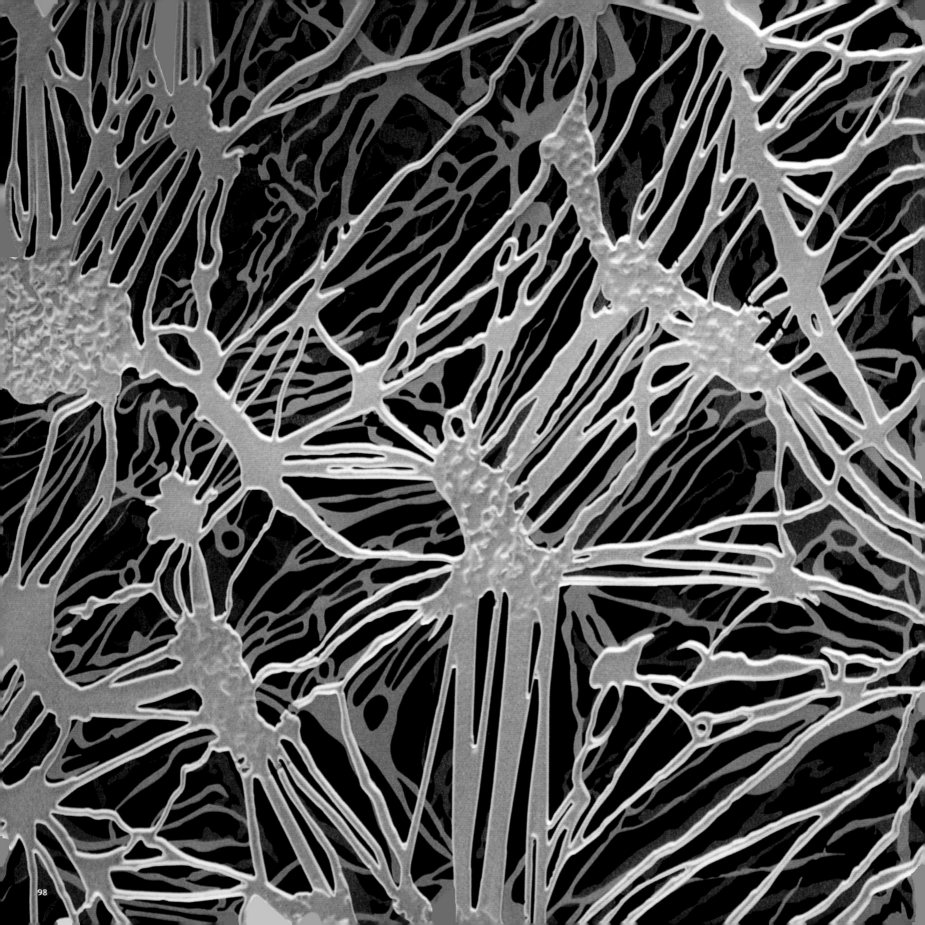

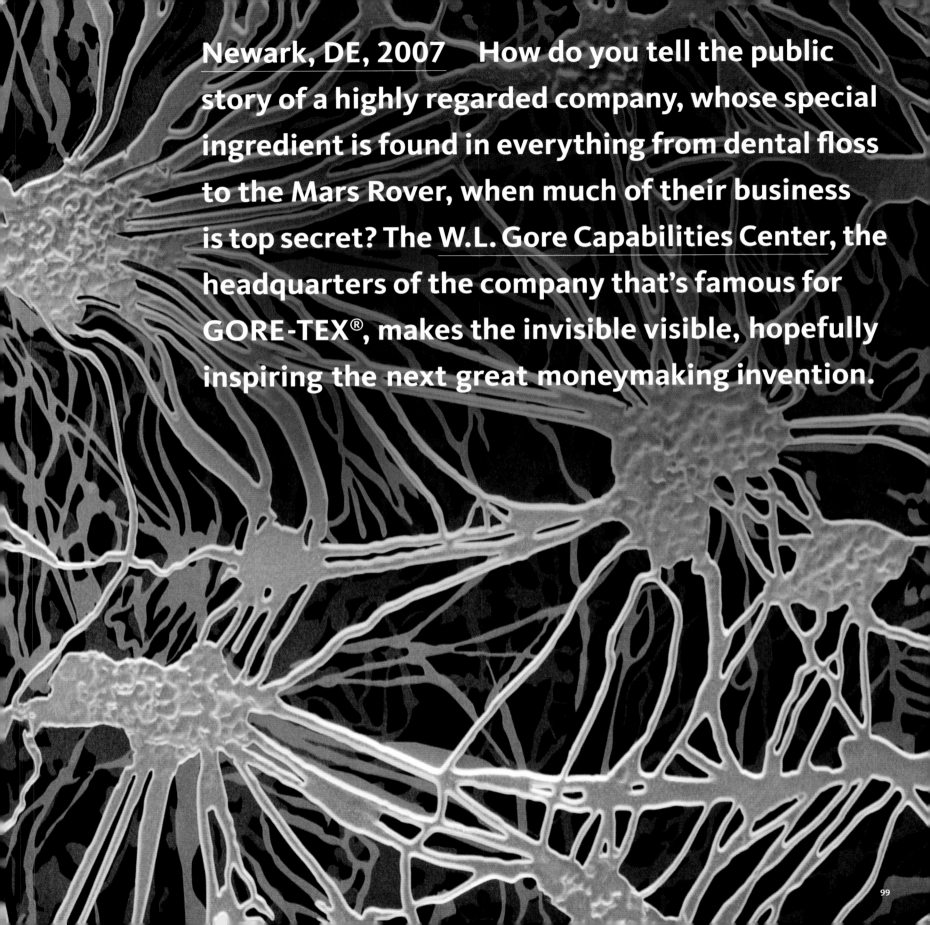

Newark, DE, 2007   How do you tell the public story of a highly regarded company, whose special ingredient is found in everything from dental floss to the Mars Rover, when much of their business is top secret? The W.L. Gore Capabilities Center, the headquarters of the company that's famous for GORE-TEX®, makes the invisible visible, hopefully inspiring the next great moneymaking invention.

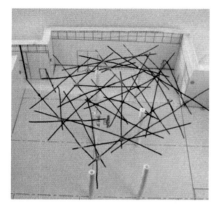

The open space for the exhibit, designed by Homsey Architects, offered great creative potential. We explored scores of three-dimensional models—some geometric, others more organic—to determine how best to tell the story of the Gore brand. Named the W.L. Gore Capabilities Center, it was built to inspire customers to use Gore products and services, while also providing a facility for media relations, recruiting, and training.

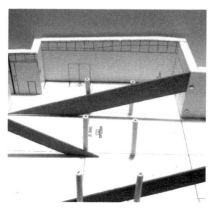

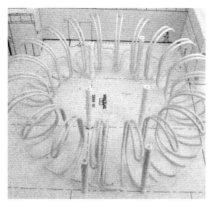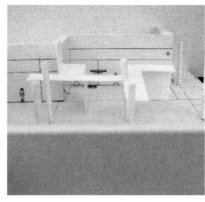
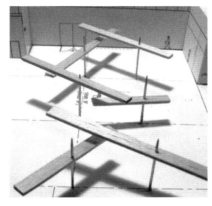
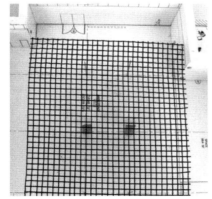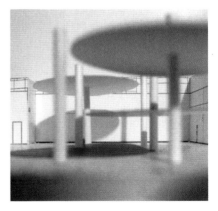

The decades of success for Gore have been built on the innovative use of a miraculous molecule called polytetrafluoroethylene, or PTFE. When magnified by an electron microscope, PTFE resembles a vast web of fibers that is essential to the hundreds of products they make for thousands of uses. This was a complex story to tell. The final hexagonal plan leads the visitor through a six-part narrative, a series of "conversation stations" that feature Gore's highly admired technical and analytical process for product creation and testing. Using diagrams, models, and digital displays, Gore can now have more productive sales conversations with customers. I told Leslie that learning about all the products they make, for industries as diverse as healthcare, aerospace, and textiles, was like getting a master's degree in engineering.

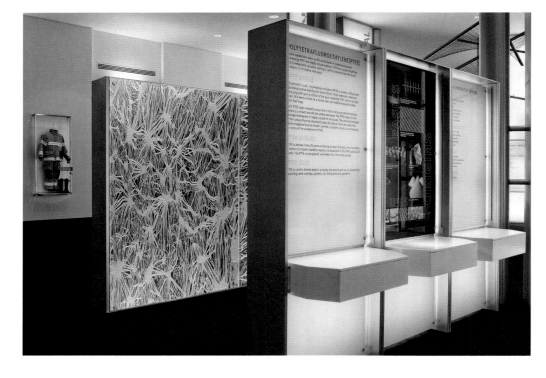

New York, NY, 1999 As they were preparing to open a new high-profile New York headquarters in Rockefeller Center, <u>Christie's</u>, the legendary auction house, asked us to rethink their global brand identity. That meant listening to input from over 100 sales offices in 33 countries, 12 focus groups, and one billionaire owner.

Our branding program was applied to Christie's locations around the world. We started with a nip-and-tuck face-lift of the 250-year-old cameo portrait of James Christie, established an official and custom "Christie's red," and applied it to auction invitations and packaging. The most visible element of the program was the design of a 100-foot-long window display system for the Rockefeller Center headquarters, to generate excitement about upcoming auctions using large-scale banners and images. We made this legendary company young again, just in time for the millennium.

Rockville Centre, NY, 2010 The website we created for **Carnegie Fabrics**, the textile and wall-covering firm, lets architects and designers flip through virtual "racks" of products and see exactly how that striped or polka-dot pattern will look on a side chair, lounger, or wall. These online innovations led to an average of 20,000 hits per month on the site—and a spike in orders.

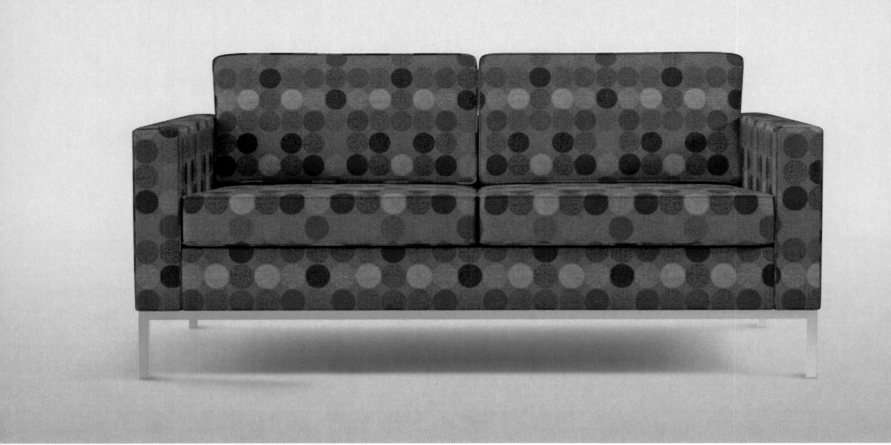

Carnegie

The beauty of this project was the close collaboration with the CEO of Carnegie Fabrics throughout the process. He had noticed dwindling face-time interaction among salespeople, designers, and buyers, which inspired him to take the company's showroom and their extensive line of fabrics online. Their beautiful textiles simply deserved a better tool to reach their customers.

The redesigned website features several ways to browse Carnegie's collections: by color, by pattern, by end use, and by designer. In addition, the site offers an assortment of over 1,000 products, simplified by detailed categorization and "In Use" features that allow customers to virtually try fabrics on sample furnishings. The bright white design of the site lends an air of precision and provides the ideal background to complement the cool, modern aesthetic of the Carnegie line.

The opening page of the site features a large-scale recreation of the Carnegie brand identity. Working with their existing Arial typeface, we transformed the eight letters of the Carnegie name into "windows" through which details of their colorful fabrics appeared. This refresh of their identity was later more broadly applied to advertisements as well.

Los Angeles, CA, 2010 Technically, our assignment was to create a signage system for the Natural History Museum of Los Angeles County and help people navigate its huge, dark, and dusty complex of buildings. But the real goal was to put a new face on the museum to increase attendance and fundraising—both of which happened. When design works, money follows.

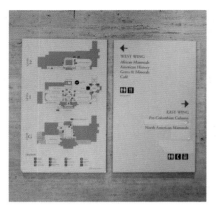

MAIN GALLERY SIGNS

Present sign area used for gallery I.D. too small

Name only

Proposal increase in sign size: architectural scale.

include collection image

WAYFINDING MAPS AT ENTRANCE HALL

Present scale is not effective

Enlarge sign

for larger maps and "billboard" images from the collection

Leslie initially made contact with Kim Baer, a Los Angeles, California-based designer whom the museum had commissioned to develop an identity and brand strategy in advance of a major five-year renovation. Baer asked us to help translate the graphic personality of her design into three dimensions in the form of a desperately needed signage system. Our photographic audit revealed that the existing buildings and signs were a terribly confusing maze of almost 100 years of incongruous architectural styles. In our early sketches, I proposed to Leslie that the big idea was to design a signage system around larger-than-life photographs of artifacts from the collection. Clearly this was a case for "weapons of mass distraction" to keep visitors focused on the best the museum had to offer.

Our scope expanded to designing a new visitors' reception area and new furnishings and information graphics for the admission and membership desks. From rough sketches to technical drawings, we continued to refine our concepts to make navigating the museum clear and easy, employing maps and images that created landmarks that visitors could reference when planning their tour of the building.

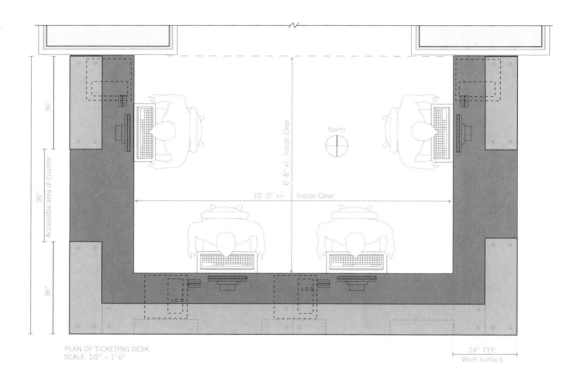

PLAN OF TICKETING DESK
SCALE: 1/2" = 1'-0"

QuartzStone image shown here for general reference only. Exact spec. T.B.D.

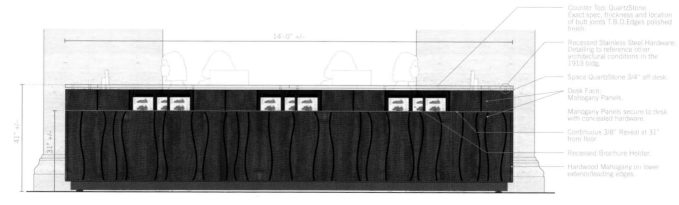

SOUTH ELEVATION OF TICKETING DESK
SCALE: 1/2" = 1'-0"

Counter Top: QuartzStone. Exact spec, thickness and location of butt joints T.B.D. Edges polished finish.

Recessed Stainless Steel Hardware: Detailing to reference other architectural conditions in the 1913 bldg.

Space QuartzStone 3/4" off desk.

Desk Face: Mahogany Panels.

Mahogany Panels secure to desk with concealed hardware.

Continuous 3/8" Reveal at 31" from floor.

Recessed Brochure Holder.

Hardwood Mahogany on lower exterior/leading edges.

188"

32.5"

28" +/−
Eq. to opposite

28" +/−
Eq. to opposite

8'-0"

4"

48"

1 3/4"

3"

8'-6" Visible height of banner

8'-0"

3"

1 3/4"

27"

ADA cane sweep

NATURAL
HISTORY
MUSEUM
LOS ANGELES COUNTY

Welcome!

← African Mammals
American History
Gems and
Minerals

→ North American
Mammals
Insect Zoo
Fin Whale Passage
Age of Mammals

Photo Panel:
Material: ARTEX flame
retardant polyester fabric.
Mfg. by seemee® Insight.
Exact product
specifications to be
provided.

ARTEX mounts to
smooth-face rigid
substrate with wrapped
edges.

Typography Banner:
Material: GRID MESH
flame retardant polyester
fabric. Mfg. by Dazian.
Exact product
specifications to be
provided.

Slotted Steel tube:
1 3/4" dia. Ends capped
Tubes seq'd. at top and
bottom. All surfaces of
tube, caps, brackets
painted finish.
Color: Gun Metal Grey

Adjustable attachment
detail must allow for
tightening of Mesh
Banners.

Large-scale graphics and digital displays in the new reception area allow the museum to promote a range of programs and events on a daily basis. Entrances to permanent exhibition areas are now identified by large, billboard-style signs featuring dramatic photography suspended over entryways. Baer's choice of the Kievit typeface for the brand identity also worked well in these signage applications.

North American Mammal Hall

The signage system brings a new sense of order to the museum. The bold use of photographs of collection specimens draws visitors to major exhibitions. The goal of our collaboration with Baer and the museum was to produce a holistic identity for the museum and convey its mission to "inspire wonder, discovery, and responsibility for our natural and cultural worlds." The generosity of others is the lifeblood of any cultural institution. Now, when the museum administration engages prospective benefactors for fundraising purposes, they can literally point to the new signage system as real evidence of the exciting improvements at the museum and encourage donors to play their part in its future.

Leslie and I are both fascinated by the natural world. It's thrilling when a scientist shows you a 30,000-year-old skull. With 35 million objects in the Natural History Museum's collection, this kind of experience happens every day. Our goal for the signage system was to share the excitement.

New York, NY, 2003   "If your firm were a tree, what kind of tree would it be?" That's one of the unexpected questions we asked the venerable white-shoe law firm Cadwalader, Wickersham & Taft while creating a new identity to shake up their stodgy image. When they chose "redwood," we knew they were ready for a bold step forward.

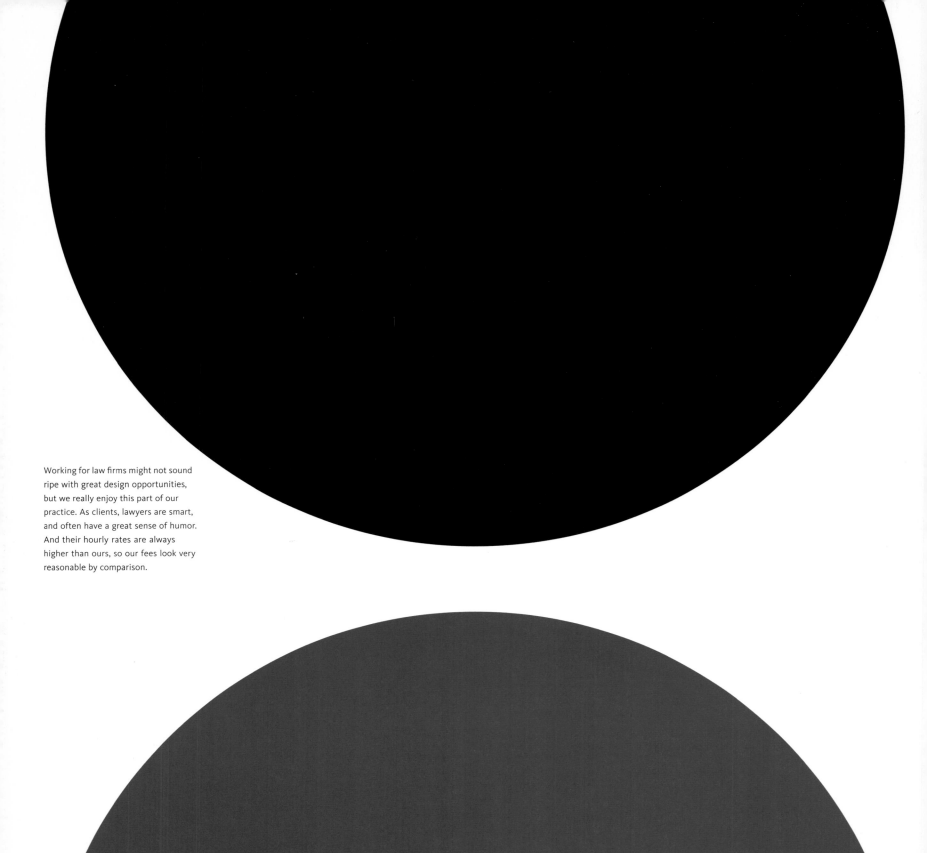

Working for law firms might not sound
ripe with great design opportunities,
but we really enjoy this part of our
practice. As clients, lawyers are smart,
and often have a great sense of humor.
And their hourly rates are always
higher than ours, so our fees look very
reasonable by comparison.

One of America's oldest law firms, Cadwalader, Wickersham & Taft's reputation reflected its august history but didn't communicate the energetic spirit of a new generation of management. We began by discarding the existing logo and created a new design program we called "color wrapped in black-and-white." Adding bold color and geometric shapes to recruiting promotions such as shopping bags and luggage tags helped express a new energy for a firm that dates back to 1792.

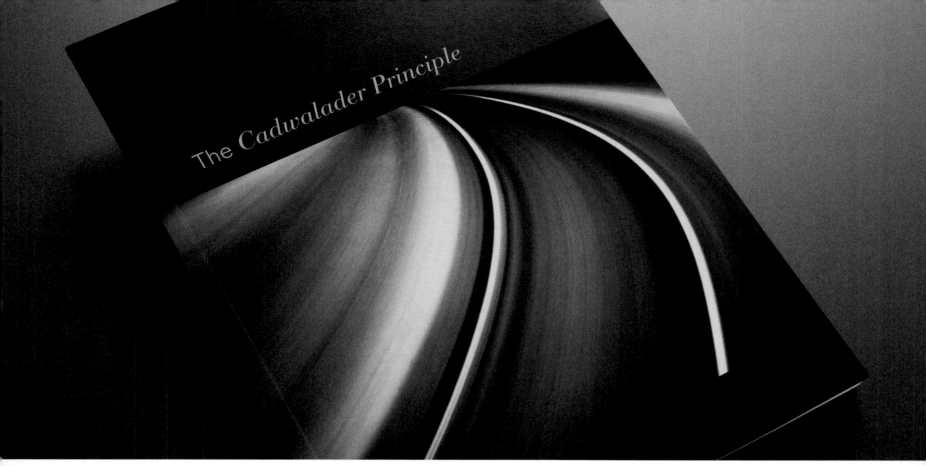

We simplified the firm's name and designed the crisp logotype "Cadwalader"
in Bodoni that, along with Helvetica
as a secondary font, made the program
adaptable to both contemporary and
conservative applications for marketing
their practice areas and attracting
new lawyers to the firm.

CADWALADER

$E=mc^2$
a small amount of mass can
generate enormous energy

CASE STUDY

2

Reengineering the Future

Cadwalader's
distinguished
complex bankru
many of the mos
history. With lead
and U.K., our multi-
to quickly resolve t
in cross-border restru

The Conservation of Essential Energy

British Energy operates a majority of
the U.K.'s nuclear power stations, gen-
erating nearly one-fifth of the electricity
that Great Britain needs to turn on its
lights every morning.

Cadwalader helped British Energy
keep that energy flowing by complet-
ing a high-profile—and often highly
charged—government-sponsored re-
structuring effort, following the publicly
traded utility's near financial collapse.

Representing a group of British E
bondholders, Cadwalader le
tions to **protect the c**
meet challengi
requiremen
estab'

proposals—Cadwa
Energy meet a stric
imposed deadline, n
agreement with all cre
we managed the mas
tion effort necessary
deal and earn final appr
European Union.

Led by
en

RIO RIO RIO

RIO RIO RIO

RIO RIO RIO RIO RIO

RIO RIO RIO RIO RIO

RIO RIO RIO RIO RIO RIO

RIO RIO RIO IBM RIO RIO RIO RIO RIO

RIO RIO RIO RIO RIO RIO RIO RIO

RIO RIO RIO RIO RIO RIO RIO RIO RIO RIO

RIO RIO RIO RIO RIO RIO RIO RIO RIO RIO

RIO RIO RIO RIO RIO RIO RIO RIO RIO RIO RIO RIO RIO

RIO RIO RIO RIO RIO RIO RIO RIO RIO RIO RIO RIO

128

RIO RIO RIO RIO RIO RIO RIO RIO RIO IBM RIO RIO RIO

RIO RIO RIO RIO RIO RIO RIO RIO RIO RIO RIO

As a young designer, I was doubly excited about creating a poster announcing the destination for an IBM conference for top salespeople: First, because what designer doesn't love creating posters, and second, because Leslie and I had been hired by a major corporation and design patron. I didn't get to go to Rio, but I did win a gold medal for the design.

RIO   RIO   RIO   RIO
RIO   RIO   RIO
RIO   RIO   RIO   RIO   RIO
RIO RIO RIO   RIO   RIO   RIO
RIO RIO   RIO RIO RIO   RIO RIO   RIO
RIO RIO RIO RIO RIO   RIO RIO   RIO RIO
RIO RIO RIO RIO RIO RIO RIO RIO RIO RIO   RIO
RIO RIO RIO IBM RIO RIO RIO RIO RIO RIO RIO RIO
RIO RIO RIO RIO RIO RIO RIO RIO   RIO RIO RIO
RIO RIO RIO RIO RIO RIO RIO IBM RIO RIO RIO RIO
RIO RIO RIO RIO RIO RIO RIO RIO RIO RIO RIO RIO
RIO RIO RIO RIO RIO RIO RIO RIO RIO RIO RIO RIO

IBM

IBM World Trade
Americas/Far East
Corporation

Convención
Latino Americana
Marzo 26-29, 1980

I interpreted Rio's famous Sugarloaf Mountain in a colorful, "pixelated" typographic illustration that evoked IBM's iconic punch cards. Recognizing that both RIO and IBM have three letters was one of those creative lucky breaks that designers love. As a visual game, I randomly inserted the IBM initials into the pattern as a "Where's Waldo?" challenge to find the company's name. It's crazy to think that I pasted in each bit of type by hand—as this project long predated desktop computers.

New York, NY, 2005   Call it survival of the fittest. Our relationship with Morgan Stanley has outlasted three CEOs and two recessions. The firm wanted to move beyond understated materials to a company-wide system that reflected Morgan Stanley's intellectual capital. Our crowning achievement was redesigning the logotype and brand pattern to suggest the visual motion of stock tickers. Building off the past, we set the stage for the future.

The most visible example of our work is the sign that towers over Morgan Stanley's headquarters, taking its rightful place among other major global brands in Manhattan's Times Square. Thirty-feet high, in ten hues of blue, the sign gives Morgan Stanley a modern, refreshed look. Every letter in the new logotype was hand-drawn to create a unique corporate signature. We believe that when you are blessed with a great name, you should have the confidence to let it speak for itself. The quietly confident brand pattern is sized for use across all media, ranging from giant applications like signage, to medium formats like a shopping bag, to a micro application like the Morgan Stanley debit card.

If the 1980s were all about the development of corporate identities and their consistent application, the 1990s were about designing unified visual and editorial systems across the thousands of communications a company produces each year. Managing complex, large-scale assignments like this one for Morgan Stanley was nothing new to me. Unlike Ken, I like this kind of challenge. You need a clear balance of logic and aesthetics to bring greater insight, meaning, and clarity to financial data. My goal has always been to make content more compelling and more accessible so readers can quickly find what's of interest.

Morgan Stanley then decided to launch a family of debit cards to expand and deepen their relationship with individual investors. We designed the card and its launch campaign to help customers "be as wise in their spending as they are in their investing." The card took top-of-wallet status and became an icon for the emotional connection that individuals have with Morgan Stanley.

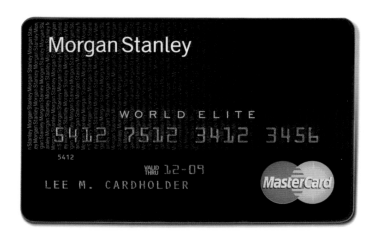

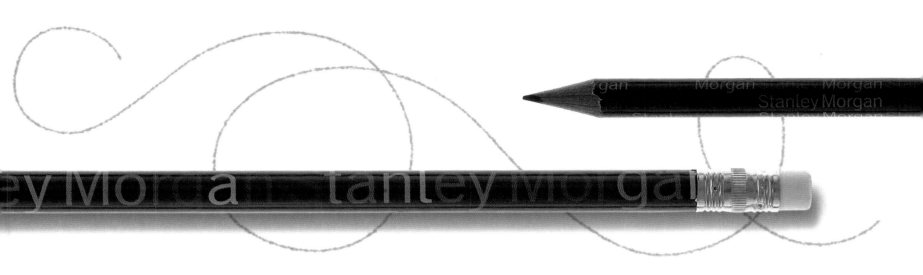

New York, NY, 1996 Receptionists used to answer the phone, "Good morning—ICF, Unika Vaev, Nienkamper." Renaming the company was a must. We came up with a design system that integrated three distinct furniture and textile lines under the single umbrella brand of the ICF Group. I remember Leslie saying to me, "These products are so beautiful they could sell themselves."

ICF|group

With great European designers like Alvar Aalto and Arne Jacobsen as our inspirational mentors, we built the new ICF Group brand identity as a consolidated selling system of binders, product promotions, advertisements, and marketing materials for maximum brand coherence. Given that the ICF Group was selling contemporary furniture to a sophisticated design audience, we were given broad creative license to promote the line. For one advertising campaign, we used whimsical illustrations of customers having fun with the company's products.

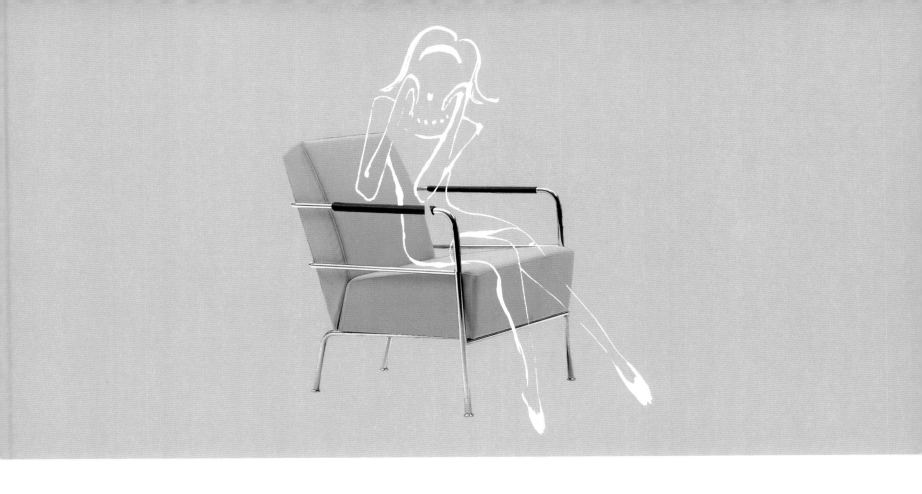

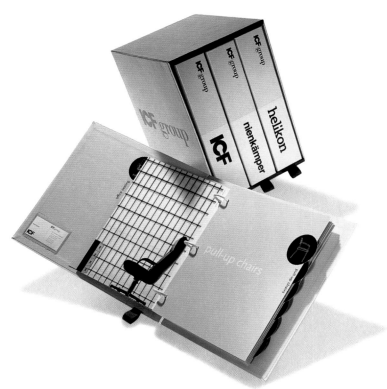

Refining the office landscape

VicoDuo designed by Vico Magistretti

Advertisements using product photography were enhanced by a soft palette of colors that were at the core of our brand identity system. Architects and interior designers responded to the new advertisements and marketing materials enthusiastically, which drove each brand to build on its product line and cultivate new creative talent. This gave the ICF Group the necessary strength to expand its base of proprietary products and to broaden the company's distribution to include retail stores. Today, the ICF Group's line of products is recognized internationally and used by businesses, professional firms, educational institutions, and the hospitality market.

ICF|group

ICF · Unika Vaev · Nienkämper · Helikon

800 237 1625
www.icfgroup.com

PHOTOGRAPHY: PETE MCARTHUR · DESIGN: CARBONE SMOLAN ASSOCIATES

Fun

What's so fun about graphic design? Plenty.

Ken and Leslie's careers have taken them on adventures they could never have imagined back in design school: being whisked to the Dominican Republic on a private helicopter while working on the eco-luxury resort Tropicalia; playing blackjack at the legendary Monte Carlo Casino with the developer of the ironically named Angst Hotel, all in the name of research.

Sure, they love the travel. But the most enjoyable thing for both partners is the work itself. "Fun is at the heart of being a creative person," says Leslie. "We are equally creative, but in very different ways. I find sweating the details to be fun. Ken likes the big, broad strokes. He loves the art part. He thinks in pictures; I think in words." Ken interjects, "I like stories, too, though I look at them through a visual lens. Obviously, I want things to look very beautiful."

Both find enjoyment in collaboration. "I'm Tom Sawyer; Ken's the Pied Piper," says Leslie. "I like getting a group of people together to run off with me and execute my vision. Ken's always getting people in the studio enthusiastic about trying new things, or saying, 'I know we've always done it this way but let's shake things up.'" Ken continues, "That's the heart of the design business. Embracing the unknown is what gets me to the studio every day."

They have a good time with their clients, too. "When we're ironing out a contract with a new client, they always say, 'Let's wrap this up quickly so we can get to the fun part,'" says Ken. "What's most fun for me is seeing their reaction to an idea you never thought they'd go for or didn't see coming. The drier and more buttoned-up the client, the more fun they have playing along in the creative process." The enjoyment is mutual. "Clients often say that the most fun they have at work is when we come in to make a presentation. It's like Christmas. The fun for us is seeing their faces and how excited they get," says Leslie. "I also have fun watching their faces when Leslie tells them it's going to cost millions to produce," adds Ken.

That's Ken's sense of humor at work.

Ken: I really wish I were funnier.

Leslie: Don't let him fool you. He's plenty funny already. He has a very quick repartee that I wish I had.

Ken: I have an inexhaustible appetite for fun but I don't think I'm funny.

Leslie: Yes he is. In contrast, my husband says I have no sense of humor.

Ken: Leslie doesn't crack jokes every day at work, but she does have great comedic timing. She can casually drop a line that is just a riot.

Leslie: Given the seriousness of so many of our projects, funniness isn't necessarily an asset. But I do think we employ wit very well in our work.

Ken: I agree. Wit—visual or verbal—works really well for our clients. It's like a laugh track for business. Humor is just another tool in our arsenal of design skills. If we can introduce a sense of lightheartedness into a project in a way that works, we go for it.

Let the fun begin.

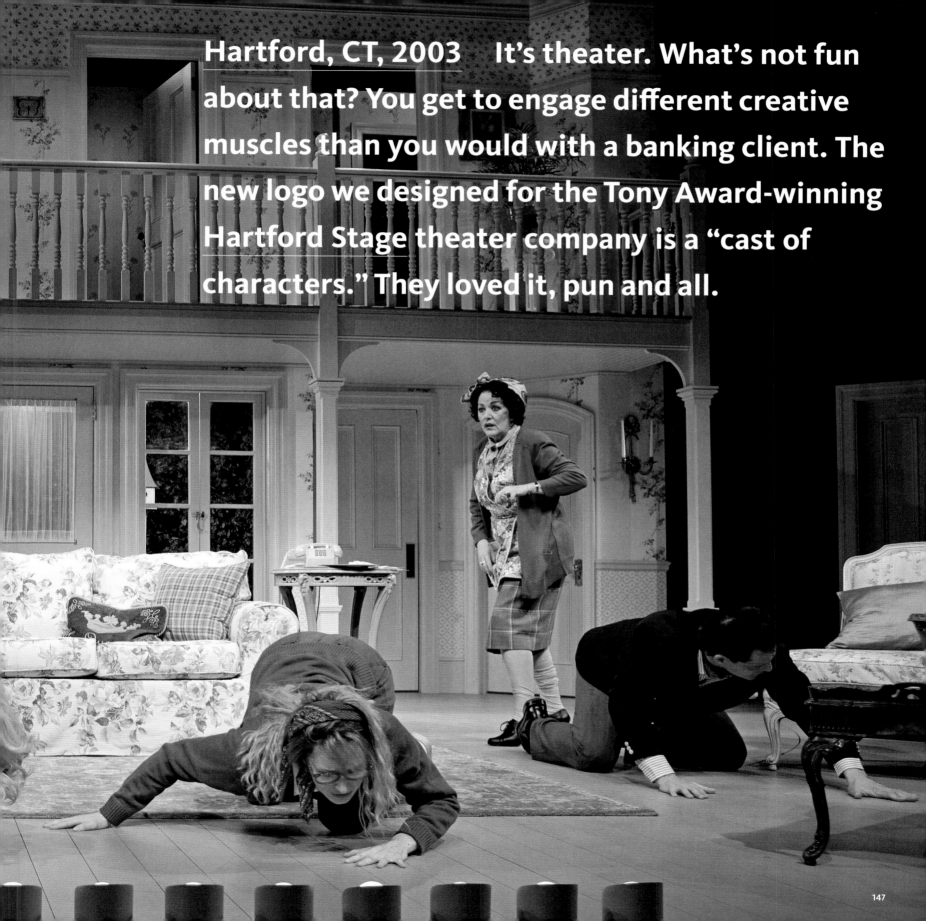

Hartford, CT, 2003 It's theater. What's not fun about that? You get to engage different creative muscles than you would with a banking client. The new logo we designed for the Tony Award-winning Hartford Stage theater company is a "cast of characters." They loved it, pun and all.

From the moment we walked into the theater, we knew this project would be fun. The entire company, from the artistic director to the head of marketing, had a great sense of humor, in spite of the daunting repertoire of solemn work by Tennessee Williams, Edward Albee, and the Bard.

The three-syllable name gave us the chance to juggle the type into a compact logo featuring a playful layering of type and colors placed solidly on a square field. The flexible color system allows the company to select a palette best suited to the mood of a particular play.

As for the "editorial voice" of the brand, the entire scripted history of theater offered endless possibilities, such as Shakespeare's "All the world's a stage" on the back of their business card.

all th

all th

all th,
world,

BOX OFFICE 8

BOX OFFICE 860-527-5151

HARt.
forD
STAGE

Ma
PUBL   MANAGER
mark   r@hartfordstage.org

TEL 860-244-0180 x247   50 Church Street
FAX 860-244-0183   Hartford, CT 06103

Cohoes, NY, 1994   We decided to re-imagine the classic fairy tale of Cinderella as a fashion feature in order to sell Mohawk paper to a sophisticated design audience. In our version, Cinderella is a bit whiny, and the evil stepmother isn't really all that evil.

The model, the make-up artist, the hair
and fashion stylists, and photographers
Rodney Smith and James Wojcik all
worked for peanuts to help create a
modern version of this classic fantasy.
I was very involved in directing
the imagery, while Ken wrote pithy
headlines and finessed the layouts.

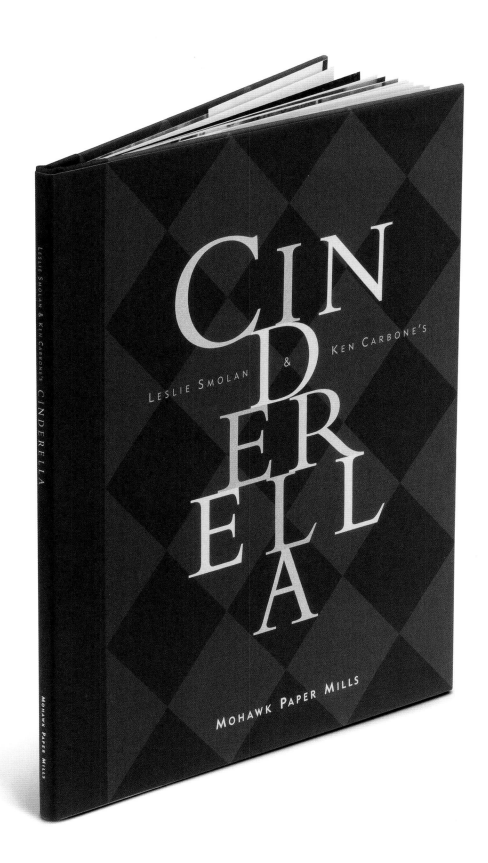

Like many fairy tales, this story has the power to enchant us every time we hear it. A hardcover book with sumptuous duotone and tritone printing ensured it would be a keeper. I consulted Richard Benson, the head of the art department at Yale University. He is a master of black-and-white images, so we met in his darkroom to talk about printing and separations. I learned a lot from him and used it to push the printer to achieve results none of us thought were possible.

Cinderella needed to look both ordinary and beautiful, so I cast Elizabeth Melcher, a friend and computer programmer, in the starring role. James Caruso, a hairstylist in the entertainment business, came with long hair for Cinderella's tresses. Regina Harris, who has worked for *Vogue* and *Vanity Fair*, did the makeup and also doubled as Cinderella's fairy godmother, and fashion stylist Magdalena Sprudin selected fantastic clothes from Isaac Mizrahi, Jean Paul Gaultier, and Vivienne Westwood.

Cinderella tells us the story of how changes in a family affect its members. Having recently become a stepmother myself, I saw this as an opportunity to tell the story in a new way. The text by Dana Wickware, a man, is written like a diary from Cinderella's point of view. It perfectly captures her self-involvement, and shows that reality is so often a matter of perspective. In our version of this tale, both Cinderella and her stepmother have happy endings.

all work

I'm exhausted. Today, I've scrubbed the tub *and* the kitchen floor *and* made the beds *and* gone to the market *and* cooked the dinner. My stepmother and stepsisters do nothing around the house, and I do everything. The three of them treat me like a servant. I don't think they mean to be cruel: but they were alone for so long, and struggled so hard, that they seem to have lost the habit of caring about others.

I've kept house for my father since my mother died, and the two of us were always happy together. But now, with the demands made on him by my stepmother and her daughters, he has nothing – neither time nor love – left for me. I've become invisible to him.

no play

El Seibo, Dominican Republic, 2009 Branding the 6,000 acres of brilliant green jungle and white-sand beaches that would one day become Tropicalia, a luxurious eco-friendly resort, was an adventure worthy of Indiana Jones.

Tropicalia, an environmentally and socially responsible tourism and real estate development of the Cisneros Group of Companies, aspires to become one of the most exclusive resorts in the Caribbean. It has the admirable mission of positioning the Dominican Republic as a destination for eco-friendly high-end tourism while supporting the development of surrounding communities.

Our branding program was applied across a range of print, digital, and 3-D formats, and had three major visual components: a unique brandmark composed of lyrical modern typography; a colorful interpretation of palm tree bark for the brand pattern; and photographs that capture the natural beauty of the landscape with a sophisticated sense of style.

TROPI
CALIA

REPÚBLICA
DOMINICANA

Our elaborate photo shoot captured a glamorous vision of the future. Guests will be able to immerse themselves in a landscape of breathtaking natural beauty—a diverse ecosystem ranging from towering mountains, to an inland lagoon lined with mangroves, to white-sand beaches bordered by coconut groves. The amenities will stick to a minimalist, low-impact philosophy that calls for elegant, understated architecture. Casa Tropicalia, the beach resort and spa on the property, was designed by the French interior architect Christian Liaigre and will be managed by Auberge Resorts.

During this project, "field research" took on a whole new meaning. We were treated to the same level of service, comfort, and adventure that future guests would enjoy, from being flown to the property by private helicopter, to the surprise of having a sumptuous meal miraculously appear on the mountaintop overlooking the turquoise sea beyond.

Our branding work also included the communications for Fundación Tropicalia, headquartered in the neighboring town of Miches, which carries out programs that contribute to the development and prosperity of the local community. A key mandate for the Cisneros Group is that corporate leadership be considered a social mission.

To communicate the deeply personal nature of the project, we created a book to tell the story of Tropicalia, using the vision and voice of the family, for whom doing well in business and doing good for the world are not mutually exclusive. The family's mission to change the world certainly changed us in the process.

MY FATHER TAUGHT ME that the world is full of possibilities – big ideas, big projects. From my mother, I learned to do everything with conviction – to trust my instincts, to act with style. I know that with great opportunities, come great responsibilities and that setting good examples is one of life's noblest actions. Even the smallest detail reflects this marriage of duty and excellence. I don't have to adapt, copy or compromise. I have resources, freedom, and a determination to continue along the path my parents began. This project is about creating the unexpected. That is the true legacy of our family.

MI PADRE ME ENSEÑÓ que el mundo está lleno de posibilidades – grandes ideas y grandes proyectos. De mi madre, aprendí a hacer todo con convicción, a confiar en mis instintos, a hacer las cosas con estilo. Sé que toda gran oportunidad implica una enorme responsabilidad y que dar buenos ejemplos es una de las acciones más nobles en la vida. Esta comunión de deber y excelencia está presente hasta en el detalle más pequeño. No tengo que adaptarme, seguir a nadie ni limitarme. Tengo recursos, libertad y absoluta determinación para continuar el camino trazado por mis padres. Tropicalia quiere crear lo inesperado. Ese es el verdadero legado de nuestra familia.

24

New York, NY, 1997   Working tête-à-tête with photographer Howard Schatz to make *Passion & Line* a great book about dancers was a creative tango. I went old-school and sketched out every spread to choreograph the pacing of Schatz's limber images of dancers. Since Leslie is the true master when it comes to photography, I was thrilled she let me design this book.

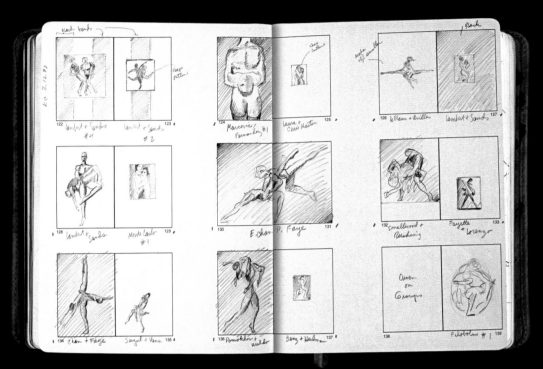

This book offered an interesting creative challenge. The good news was there were so many beautiful images to choose from. The bad news was there were so many beautiful images to choose from. Editing the photographs was the first task. For me, doing pencil drawings of each spread was the fastest way to see how the images would best work as a "book" and not just a photographic portfolio. What about the cover? Schatz chose the final image and I absolutely loved it. All I had to do was add the type.

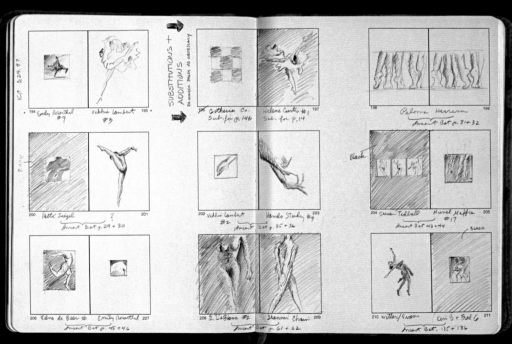

Most of the book contains black-and-white images, so pale purple as an accent seemed to provide the best color complement. I approached the type with tasteful restraint. After all, this was Howard Schatz's book of photographs, not Ken Carbone's book of typography.

that their grace is magic, not muscle.

The secret of **women** who dance is the illusion

The dynamic range of Schatz's work is impressive. From delicate sensuality to explosive theatrics, his brilliant photographs of what dancers can do physically and artistically were great fun to work with when designing this book.

Chicago, IL, 1995   Both Leslie and I have music in our backgrounds. For her it was the oboe; for me, the guitar. Part of our research to design the new logo for the Chicago Symphony Orchestra was to tour Carnegie Hall in New York. As I stood on the stage, awestruck, I couldn't resist striking middle 'C' on the beautiful Steinway piano next to me. I still tell my kids that I once played Carnegie Hall.

When we began our design study for the logo, we played with a shape that was familiar to us: the curves of a bass clef. By flipping the clef symbol and tweaking its shape, we got a beautifully stylized capital C for Chicago, which we placed on an abstracted musical staff. The scope of the project included everything from print, to signage, to branded merchandise such as T-shirts.

Henry Fogel
President

220 South Michigan Avenue
Chicago, IL 60604-2508
Telephone 312.294.3210
Facsimile 312.294.3329
fogel@chicagosymph.org

New York, NY, 2011 Today, everyone wants to work at Facebook or Google. Our mission was to convince them to work for Morgan Stanley. So we created a bold, contemporary, "you-focused" global recruiting campaign featuring models shot by a young photographer on the campus of Princeton University. Confidence is compelling.

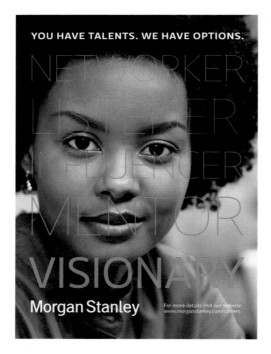

YOU HAVE TALENTS. WE HAVE OPTIONS.

VISIONARY

Morgan Stanley

For more details visit our website
www.morganstanley.com/careers

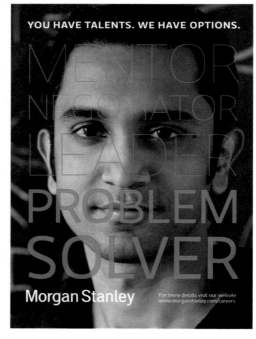

YOU HAVE TALENTS. WE HAVE OPTIONS.

PROBLEM
SOLVER

Morgan Stanley

For more details visit our website
www.morganstanley.com/careers

The mindset of recruiting has changed dramatically in the new economy. Recruits today are interested in building their resumes, not taking a job for the next 30 years. Our bold campaign, featuring large-scale black-and-white portraits by Seth Smoot, overlaid with brightly colored typographic attributes, said it all: You have talents, we have options. Let's talk.

Wanting to see the campaign in action, I told Ken I was going to sneak into a recruiting event at Columbia University. When I arrived, the faces on the posters were perfectly mirrored around the room, as were the ambitions.

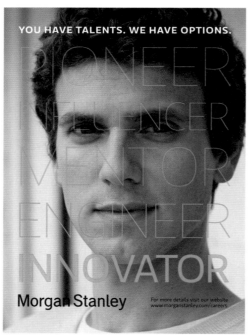

YOU HAVE TALENTS. WE HAVE OPTIONS.

INNOVATOR

Morgan Stanley

For more details visit our website
www.morganstanley.com/careers

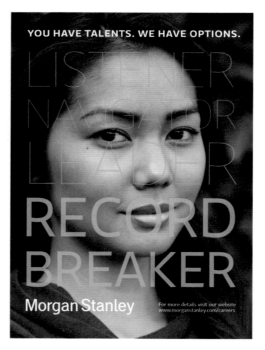

YOU HAVE TALENTS. WE HAVE OPTIONS.

RECORD
BREAKER

Morgan Stanley

For more details visit our website
www.morganstanley.com/careers

YOU HAVE TALENTS. WE HAVE OPTIONS.

MENTOR
ENGINEER
PIONEER
INFLUENCER
INNOVATOR

Morgan Stanley

For more details visit our website
www.morganstanley.com/careers

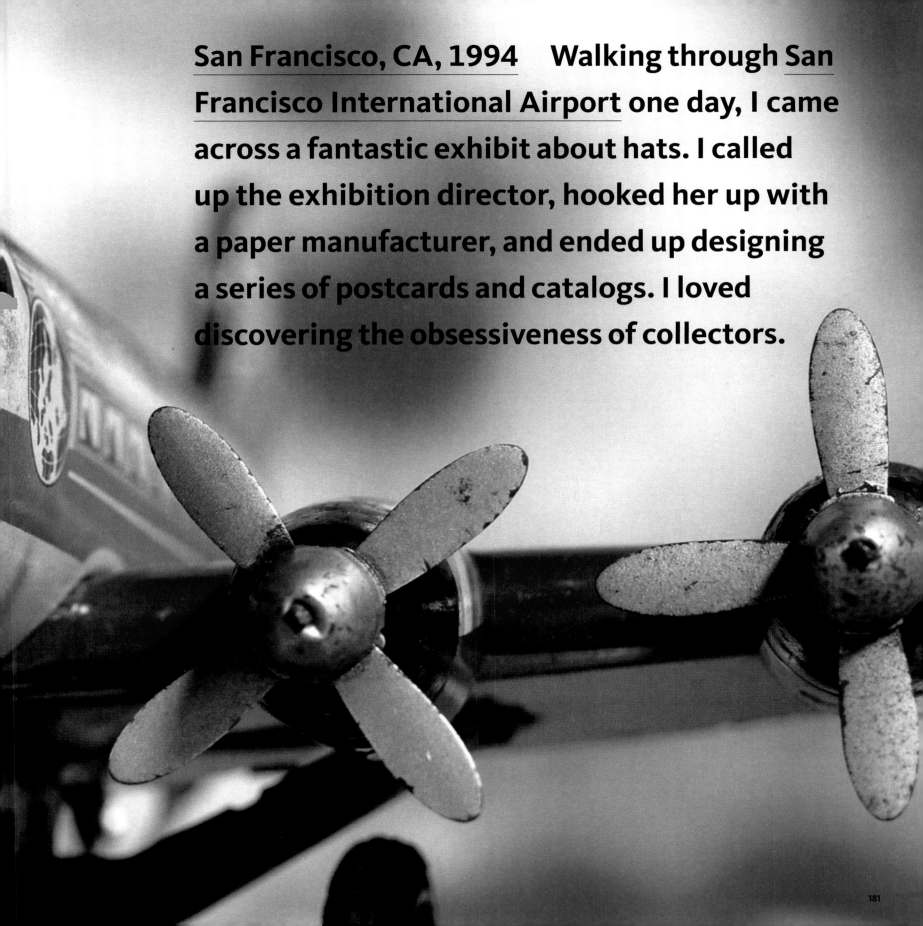

San Francisco, CA, 1994 Walking through San Francisco International Airport one day, I came across a fantastic exhibit about hats. I called up the exhibition director, hooked her up with a paper manufacturer, and ended up designing a series of postcards and catalogs. I loved discovering the obsessiveness of collectors.

TRICKY TAXIS, EARLY 1950s. MARX, UNITED STATES. LITHOGRAPHED TIN. COLLECTION OF NATHAN WILLENSKY, NEW YORK.

During the twentieth century tin toys came to dominate the world of toymaking. Made of two or more pieces stamped out by machine, they are assembled by hand using a solder or bent-tab method. They were painted by hand until the invention of offset lithography. Marx is noted for its wind-up toys. The *Tricky Taxi* was produced just prior to Marx's switch to plastic from tin. Wound with a key, it will go to the edge of a table, stop, and not fall off.

TO

THE SAN FRANCISCO AIRPORTS COMMISSION PRESENTS HAILING TAXIS · OCTOBER 1994–FEBRUARY 1995, SAN FRANCISCO INTERNATIONAL AIRPORT

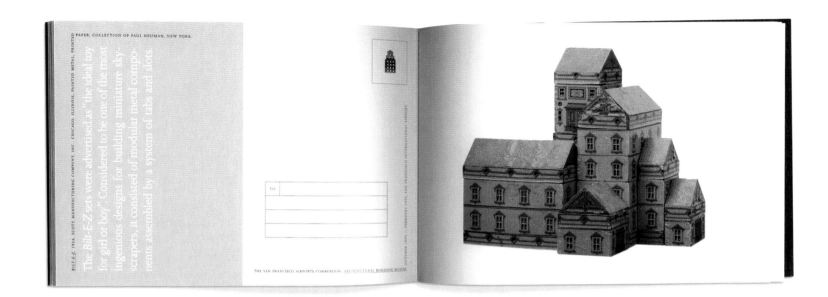

BILT-E-Z 1924, SCOTT MANUFACTURING COMPANY, INC., CHICAGO, ILLINOIS. PAINTED METAL, PRINTED PAPER. COLLECTION OF PAUL NEUMAN, NEW YORK.

The *Bilt-E-Z* sets were advertised as "the ideal toy for girl or boy." Considered to be one of the most ingenious designs for building miniature skyscrapers, it consisted of modular metal components assembled by a system of tabs and slots.

TO

THE SAN FRANCISCO AIRPORTS COMMISSION. ARCHITECTURAL BUILDING BLOCKS

OCTOBER 1994 – FEBRUARY 1996, SAN FRANCISCO INTERNATIONAL AIRPORT

Ken was impressed that I would always try to meet the collectors. Nathan Willensky's collection started when his mother gave him a cookie jar shaped like a taxi. Every nook and cranny of his tiny apartment was overflowing with his collection of over 11,000 taxi-related pieces, including 1,700 antique and contemporary toy taxis, taxi medallions, and license plates, as well as sheet music, film posters, postage stamps, board games, matchbooks, and paperweights.

Architectural Building Blocks celebrates the evolution of constructional toys and showcases an extraordinary collection of building blocks and construction sets.

patent drawings
used as graphics (end pages)

recipe wheel

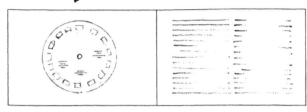

collection of European
shakers ("the cocktail abroad")

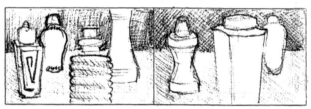

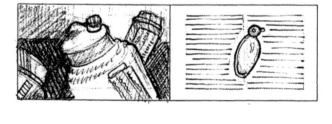

For the first four books of postcards, we selected the objects, directed the photography, illustrated the cover, designed the layout, and condensed the story of the exhibition into a brief introductory description. Later, our book of postcards evolved into full-fledged catalogs.

For the *Art Deco* catalog, I even contributed my own 1940s Herman Miller clock. Luckily for my bank account, this collection is one of one.

collection of
recipe shakers

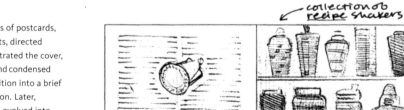

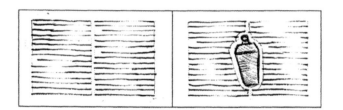

collection of
novelty shakers

glass dumbbell
shakers

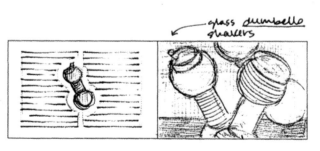

T he year was 1933, and the tempo of life was changing. Jazz was in the air; the skyscraper vaulted upwards piercing the clouds; and the airplane sped from coast to coast. While the race towards modern life had begun in the nineteenth century, it was only by the 1920s and 30s that modernity's broad and far-reaching influences took hold of everyday life. These years also saw the rise of the cocktail as a way to celebrate or escape these modern times, with the gentle rhythmic sound of the cocktail swirling in a vessel as it was shaken, not stirred. ≫—➤ To study the design and use of the cocktail shaker — an American invention — during its golden years between the two world wars reveals the developing modern life-style and an understanding of Art Deco design. Manufacturers such as Chase and Manning Bowman, attempted to capitalize on America's growing interest in the cocktail culture. They enlisted the efforts of leading industrial designers to produce sleek, modern deco-styled cocktail shakers to reflect the prosperity of the 1920s and to deflect the harsher realities of the 1930s depression.

LEFT: JUMBO AEROPLANE TRAVELING BAR, C. 1930, GERMANY, SILVER-PLATE, TOY BUILDINGS, 1930s, LOUIS MARX AND COMPANY, NEW YORK CITY, LITHOGRAPHED TIN

ART DECO AND THE COCKTAIL SHAKER

P rohibition was an extension of the Lever Food Act, passed during World War I to reduce the use of grain. This initially patriotic ruling was extended even further through the women's Suffragette movement, ending with the passage of the 19th Amendment on August 26, 1920 banning the production of all alcoholic drinks. While Prohibition remained intact for thirteen years, it had little effect on the cocktail. Mixed drinks grew in popularity not only to disguise the alcohol in the glass, but also to cover over the taste of poor quality alcohol.

≫—➤ The early years of Prohibition coincided with the rise of a new art style in France — Art Deco. The term was derived from the great 1925 Paris exhibition, *L'Exposition International des Arts Decoratifs et Industriels*. It was applied to the artistic productions of the 1920s and 1930s, when an attempt was made to unite the "fine arts" and "industrial arts". A decidedly modern style, Art Deco grew in popularity as the machine age geared into production. ≫—➤ Art Deco revolved around the increasingly rapid change brought about by industrialization and mass production, as well as the growing populations in the cities. Art Deco, while adapting elements of "high art", applied its style to objects of daily life. ≫—➤ Art Deco is not one specific style. Rather it combines a variety of art styles and influences, including Italian Futurism, Russian Constructivism, cubism, abstraction, distortion, and simplification. While stylistically diverse, Art Deco contains common elements, such as a lack of excessive decoration and the use of geometric, stylized and simplified shapes. Its ornamentation often includes stylized flowers, young maidens, geometric zigzags, chevrons and lightning bolts, often taken from the world of high fashion, Egyptology, Asia, tribal Africa, and the Ballet Russes. A pronounced influence was also the machine, with the application of streamlined design suggesting speed, taken from the principles of aerodynamics. ≫—➤ The cocktail shakers of the 1920s reflect early French Art Deco in the use of expensive materials. This can be understood when a single sterling silver cocktail shaker sold for $95. Cocktail parties grew in popularity. Art Deco, however, was much more than a style. It was symbol and expression of a new modern life.

ABOVE: COMMEMORATIVE DESK ORNAMENT, P-51 "MUSTANG" AIRPLANE, 1945, USA, CHROMED METAL

ABOVE: KODAK "BEAU BROWNIE" BOX CAMERA, 1930, DESIGNED BY WALTER DORWIN TEAGUE, EASTMAN KODAK COMPANY, ROCHESTER, NEW YORK, METAL, GLASS, LEATHER

ART DECO IN AMERICA

T he 20th century initiated a period of dramatic social changes in the United States. For women, in particular, the constraints of the Victorian era in terms of fashion and mores were cast aside. The Suffragette movement propelled women into more independent and liberated roles. The economy was booming, and the age of the flappers, complete with jazz, speakeasies, and a flamboyant, carefree life-style was evident across the country. ≫—➤ Black Thursday, October 24, 1929, would bring this affluent life-style to an end. With the stock market crash, the United States began a ten year economic depression, when few could afford a $95 sterling silver cocktail shaker. ≫—➤ By the mid 1920s, Prohibition was considered a failure by many people. On December 5, 1933, the 21st Amendment repealing Prohibition was passed, ending thirteen "dry" years. President Franklin Roosevelt toasted this event with a martini, calling for the nation to practice moderation. ≫—➤ With prohibition over, the real explosion of cocktail shakers began. The design of the Art Deco cocktail shak-

ABOVE: DESK CLOCK, 1930, HERMAN MILLER CLOCK COMPANY, ZEELAND, MICHIGAN, CHROME AND GLASS
RIGHT: DUMBBELL COCKTAIL SHAKER, C. 1932, NATIONAL SILVER DEPOSIT WARE COMPANY, NEW YORK CITY, FROSTED GLASS WITH APPLIED SILVER TRIM

WAR SHIRT AND HAT WITH TALISMANS. GHANA. COLLECTION OF THE AMERICAN MUSEUM OF NATURAL HISTORY (90.2/5732 A, B).

In West Africa, hunters and soldiers wore shirts covered with talismans. The cotton tunics and hats served as a background for the application of objects that contained sources of power. Some of these were herbal medicines, and some were charms made from parts of animals deemed to convey power or protection to the wearer. Most of the charms were leather envelopes that contained paper on which inscriptions from the Qur'an were written.

TO

TARGET KITE. C. 1942–1945. SPAULDING BROTHERS. UNITED STATES. FABRIC. THE RONALD WINSTON COLLECTION, NEW YORK.

Target kites were used by all branches of the United States armed forces for anti-aircraft gunnery practice. They were towed by slow moving aircraft, jeeps, or light trucks.

TO

THE SAN FRANCISCO AIRPORTS COMMISSION PRESENTS: PEACE   APRIL 1993 – JULY 1993, SAN FRANCISCO INTERNATIONAL AIRPORT

Peace features the collection belonging to Ronald Winston, son of diamond merchant Harry Winston, and includes over 1,200 spotter models and thousands of manuals, posters, and other World War II aircraft identification aids that helped American pilots instantly identify the silhouettes of oncoming enemy aircraft.

African Textiles reflects the cultures and history of Africa through examples of woven, printed, and beaten textiles selected from many parts of the African continent.

Meet Jerry George Elaine & Kramer

New York, NY, 1998 When we were designing a recruiting brochure for legal giant <u>Skadden Arps</u>, we discovered staffers with names like Faulkner, Rodin, Lewis, Clark, Eisenhower, and Nixon. As more "famous" names were revealed, we realized we were onto a big idea and a fun concept.

MeetPeter Paul & Mary

Skadden Arps is known as a tough, no-nonsense law firm. However, they play as hard as they work—an important message to communicate to young recruits. Our concept was to feature portraits of attorneys and staff that coincidentally bore the same names as celebrities and historical figures. After we presented the idea to the head of recruiting, there was a long pause—and then a big grin came over her face. At that moment, we knew this would be a winning campaign.

To play against the campaign's inherently humorous tone, we kept the design reserved and straight-laced, with serious black-and-white portraits and traditional Bodoni type. The *Wall Street Journal* and the legal press picked up on our entertaining approach to recruiting, and to this day it is remembered by many in the legal profession. It gave lawyers everywhere license not to take themselves so seriously.

MeetRodin

Meet
Lewis
& Clark

MeetFaulkner
Yates & Heminway

Bordighera, Italy, 2009   Would you stay at a hotel called Angst? With a guest list that once included Andrew Carnegie, Louis Comfort Tiffany, and Queen Victoria, the place must have had a certain Freudian attraction.

Bringing life back to Adolf Angst's once-grand Belle Epoque resort on the Italian Riviera took a big leap of faith. The site was a complete ruin, with many decades of weather damage and vandalism having destroyed the once fabulously ornate interiors. The entrance was marked by an historical relic, a rusted sign that read "Angst." We didn't give it a second thought: There was the inspiration for the new logo.

Adolph
ANGST

1845

L'Hotel Angst fu, tra il XIX ed il XX secolo, uno degli alberghi più prestigiosi ed eleganti. L'Hotel Angst, anche se fatiscente ed abbandonato, rimane ancora oggi un simbolo sia per i bordigotti che per i turisti, a testimonianza dell'illustre tradizione turistica di Bordighera.

Simona Marino si è laureata a Bologna con una tesi intitolata Hotel Angst A Bordighera.

We took our design cues not from the derelict building's lavish architecture, but from the lush Mediterranean gardens around it. We thought a distinctly feminine graphic language of floral motifs and subtle pastel colors applied to brochures and room amenities would help soften the impact of such a harshly forbidding name.

New York, NY, 2007 Our rebranding of <u>Bideawee</u> replaced the 100-year-old animal advocacy group's outdated logo with a modern one packed with visual wit. The "w" becomes part of the smiling face of both a cat and a dog, making lovers of both species happy. Bideawee got more online donations in the month after our web redesign was unveiled than in the entire previous year. The branding is not just cute: It works.

The name Bide-A-Wee, a Scottish term meaning "stay a while," was hard to say and remember—not to mention to type. We changed the look by removing the difficult capitalization and hyphenation. Shifting the color to magenta in the "a" made pronunciation easier, and adding the dog and cat drawing to the "w" created a logotype and symbol simultaneously.

The playfulness of the program translated easily to a number of items. Bideawee's "pet parents" now display the brand proudly on scarves and nametags, and the advertisements, posters, and website all have a fun look that helped Bideawee reach a whole new generation of prospective pet lovers. Ken has guinea pigs, but a lifetime of pet allergies prevented me from ever becoming a pet parent myself.

201

Freedom

Running a partnership comes with obvious freedoms: not having to answer to a higher power, choosing what projects to work on and with whom, "being able to walk away from things that don't meet our basic requirements of fair play and fair pay," Ken explains. "It's all about choice," offers Leslie. "We are trained as 'commercial' artists, but we also like to be able to follow our own interests and passions instead of always having to focus on the bottom line," she says.

What are those passions? For Leslie, it's photography; for Ken, "freedom to be the illustrator if I want to, because I love to draw." For both, it's important to be able to donate some of their time to nonprofits. "We've consciously built the business at a manageable scale—50 people or fewer—so we're not slaves to the overhead," notes Ken. It's easy to see free-flying

creativity in self-published projects like *The Hat Book* or the commission to design *NEO* magazine, for the Simpson Paper Company.

Nor are they bound to a signature aesthetic. "We don't have to cater to a client's expectations of an agency style. For us, nothing visual is locked down," suggests Ken. "Some designers say, 'I work with two typefaces and that's it,' which gives them a signature look that's more identifiable to clients. That makes things easier for them," says Leslie. "We go back to the creative well every time. That makes more work for us, but it keeps us nimble stylistically, which is definitely more fun."

The partners deal with the usual headaches and responsibilities of running a business: hiring good people, delivering great work, long hours. "We are free to enjoy our successes as well as our failures," adds Ken. And they were free to take back-to-back sabbaticals in 2000, much to the surprise of their design peers. While one partner was away, traveling, studying, and pursuing personal interests, the other ran the entire business. The one on sabbatical didn't check in at all—not even a single phone call. "We saw it just like professors taking a leave to recharge their batteries and re-engage with the world. When we returned to work, we had new experiences to draw on," explains Leslie.

The ultimate freedom for the partners may be their complete and total trust in each other—their marked differences as well as their complementary talents.

Leslie: I find it liberating when Ken gets up to present to a new client and just says all the right things. And if they aren't impressed enough, he will whip out a pen and draw the idea upside down so it's facing the client, just to reinforce his point.

Ken: I have the freedom to acknowledge where my real strengths are, the clarity of my ideas, and how best to articulate them.

Leslie: He's liberated by me because he knows I've got the details covered.

Ken: And Leslie knows I'm always ready to jump in if a project needs the jolt of a new idea.

Leslie: This doesn't mean Ken and I always agree. We argue because we're both so passionate.

Ken: But when we do fight, we always find a middle ground that ultimately makes the work better.

Leslie: The ultimate freedom is that we can shut this whole business down when it's no longer fun.

Ken: There is nothing wrong with closing up shop and declaring victory.

For now, the adventure continues.

New York, NY, 1993   My first foray into self-publishing, *The Hat Book* was a labor of love. Teaming up with photographer Rodney Smith to chronicle the experience, whimsy, and sense of style that hats bestow, I ended up wearing many hats: agent, producer, designer, editor, publicist, and author. The book won dozens of awards, from the Leipzig International Book Competition to the *Communication Arts* Design Competition. But most important, it won me the heart of the photographer, who is now my husband.

"Look at me!
Look at me now!" said the cat.
"With a cup and a cake
On top of my hat!" —DR. SEUSS, *THE CAT IN THE HAT*

Leading the genre of compact coffee table books, *The Hat Book* was small on size but big on production values. The book combined Smith's amazing images with extraordinarily beautiful printing on heavyweight paper. The text consists of amusing quotes and essays from unexpected literary sources, such as F. Scott Fitzgerald, Richard Bernstein, and even Dr. Seuss. Nan A. Talese at Knopf Doubleday blessed us with her imprint, and a jaunty red ribbon tied the whole package together.

The inspiration for this project was a lucky series of accidents. Flying home from a press run in Boston, I was seated next to a gentleman who owned a hat company in Pennsylvania. A shared ride to downtown Manhattan with a kamikaze cab driver cemented our friendship, so weeks later I accepted his offer to tour his 100-year-old factory. It was fabulous and very Dickensian, like being transported back in time.

Just around the same time, I'd been introduced to photographer Rodney Smith, and went to visit him at his studio in Connecticut. When I saw his stunning black-and-white pictures, I was struck by their combination of artistry and spirituality. Smith managed to capture the soul of his subjects, ranging from migrant farmers to CEOs. He was obstinately non-commercial, which felt just perfect for a new look at the experience of wearing hats. I suggested we work together and he enthusiastically agreed.

Hats

disappeared somewhere between my childhood and

my college days. Maybe it was because John Kennedy had such gorgeous hair and therefore didn't

like hats to hide it—even on that frosty day in January when he took his oath of office. He showed

us there was something liberating and democratic, something emblematic of American independence

in our going around bare headed. And so by the mid-sixties, hardly anyone wore hats, except in win-

ter to keep their ears warm. ➤ But when I was growing up in the South in the forties, most grown-

ups wore hats both indoors and out. My mother's five tall brothers lounged around the porch of

the family house, all in their creamy straw Panamas with the wide striped bands; their hats as much

a part of their daily apparel as their wide ties and the crisp white cotton shirtsleeves rolled above

their elbows. Their wives also wore hats, not just to church but whenever they went out, even to the

Like its subject, *The Hat Book* combined traditional and state-of-the-art technology. Wanting both sharpness and softness, we combined laser-sharp tritone separations with premium uncoated paper. To counteract the problem of ink spread, we used "dry-trap" printing, which leaves the ink to dry for 24 hours between each pass. The process is about four times as complicated and expensive as ordinary offset printing, but the result is stunningly rich. It's a true show-stopper and called on everything I'd ever learned about offset production, and then some. The 128-page book took five years to complete, and to this day it is one of the projects of which I'm most proud.

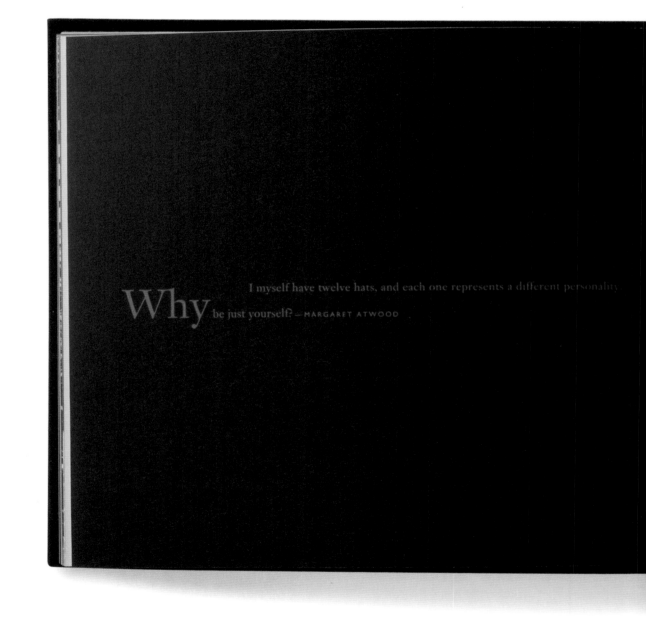

Why be just yourself? I myself have twelve hats, and each one represents a different personality. —MARGARET ATWOOD

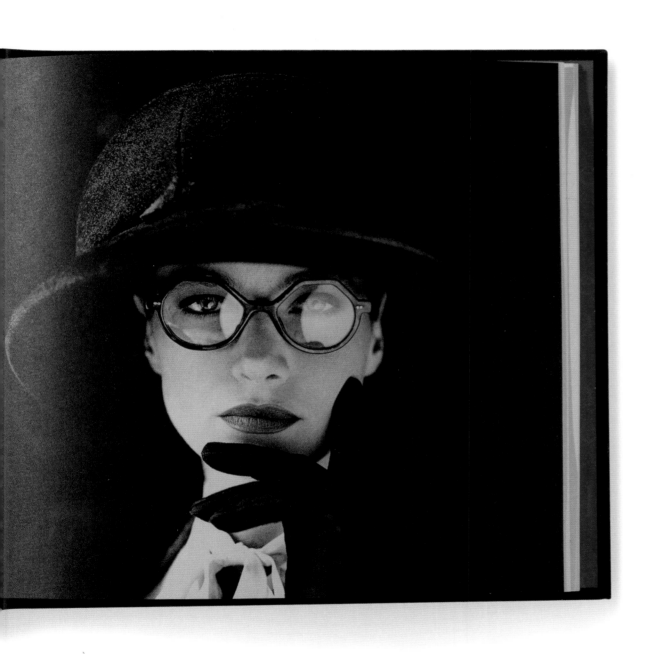

Bristol, PA, 1982   Designing a line of dinnerware for <u>Dansk</u> was a totally new experience for us. It gave us the opportunity to explore a new medium without any preconceptions. This freedom paid off when our first royalty check arrived.

**Carbone Smolan
Associates**

170 Fifth Avenue

New York NY 10010

Tel 212 807 0011

Mr. Dick Ryan
President
Dansk International Designs Ltd.
Radio Circle Road
Mount Kisco, NY 10549

November 2, 1988

Dear Mr. Ryan,

We were pleased to have a chance to sit and discuss Ditto and
the Dansk product line with you. Gabrielle's enthusiasm, and
detailed tour helped re-acquaint us, and we look forward to
developing some new applications to either Aartik or Tivoli.

I've given more thought to your question of whether Ditto is
timeless, or classical enough. I still feel it is, and
perhaps the response you've gotten is based on Dansk being
able to provide a "modern classic," which none of the other
patterns provide. If someone wants Dansk and modern, they
now have Ditto. I'd like to sit with Gabrielle, and perhaps
yourself, to discuss a new direction, which might again
appeal to a specific audience.

We also briefly discussed the development of marketing
materials for the new Dansk stores; an exciting new route for
Dansk International Designs Ltd. We look forward to working
together again.

Best,

Leslie Smolan
Principal

The goal was to offer a Danish modern design that would compete with Swid Powell, a company that was hiring architects to design tabletop items. Our design would be the first pattern to grace a new plate form created by industrial designer Larry Porcelli. With its crisp white finish and clean lines, it felt almost perfect *without* graphics. Ken let me take the lead on this project, and being ignorant about designing ceramics, I was able to ask all the "why not?" questions, such as "Why can't I wrap the color around the edge of the plate?"

TRY SMALLER —
MORE DOT.

INLAID MARBLE
ON BLACK?

F

Geometric
Dark background
light lines
Fine lacy, but
geometric

Allison

Gray center
White flange

change
surface

Matt vs gloss
White
texture

Create 3-D edge
possibly wrap
color
Possibly flange
different flange
box color?
black

or decorate
just edge

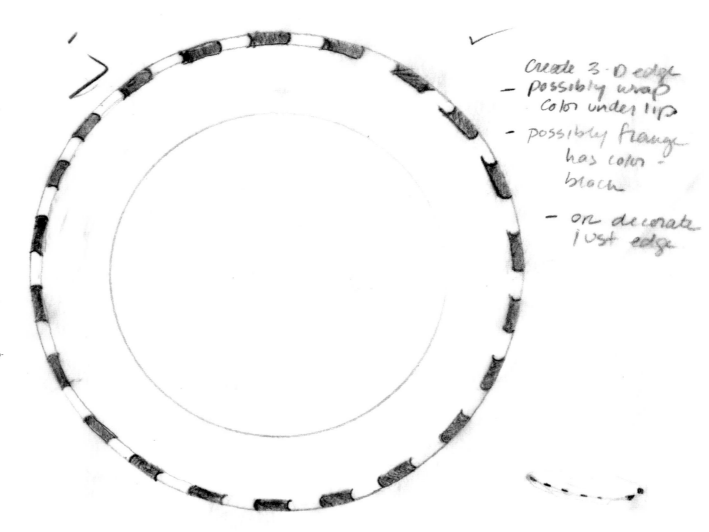

Minimalism seemed the best approach, so I focused on the edge of the plate, wondering about how to enhance the look when the china is stacked on kitchen shelves. As we moved into prototypes, it was interesting to see how a simple color shift changed the whole impression of the plate. One idea for a more upscale feel utilized a series of metallic decals in gold, silver, and bronze.

Create 3-D edge
- possibly wrap color under lip

- possibly flauge has color-block

- or decorate just edge

The final pattern, which I named "Ditto," was a classic black-and-white composition, easy to use every day or for a fancy dinner party. My favorite piece is the saucer, where the inner ring shifts to black, concealing any unsightly coffee spills.

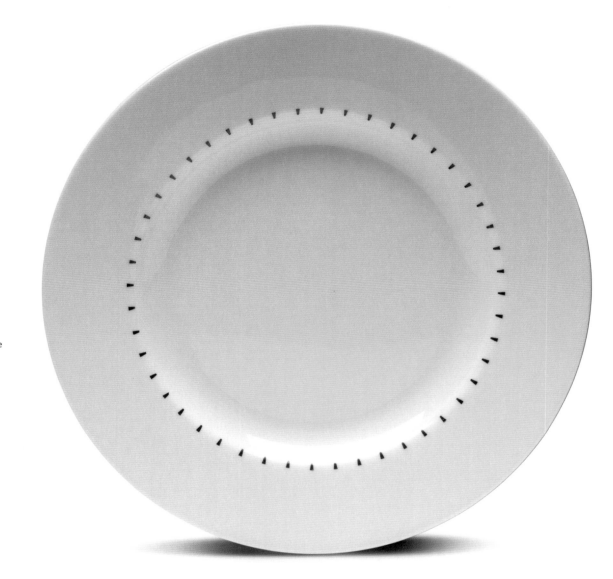

Albert Watson, "Golden Boy, New York City, 1990."

Seattle, WA, 1996 *NEO*, a magazine published by the Simpson Paper Company, was one of the most coveted graphic design projects of its time. We had total creative control to deliver a tour-de-force of printing and paper performance.

Getting to design *NEO*, a special-edition magazine targeted to designers and built around the central theme of innovation and rediscovery, was a really big deal. We wanted to highlight some of the most creative people, places, and things influencing contemporary culture, and decided to showcase people like performance artist Laurie Anderson, French architect Pierre Chareau, and fashion designer Gene Meyer, whose graphic neckties became the art for our front and back covers.

Fall 1996 | Neo: A Journal of Innovation and Rediscovery | Volume 5

neo

SIMPSON

We were being paid to experiment. Here, we dissected one of Albert Watson's famous photographs to explain how the negatives had to be prepared, the inks selected, and the correct sequence of offset plates in order to recreate a masterpiece on uncoated paper. With our help, *NEO* became a technical primer to help designers push the limits of printing technology.

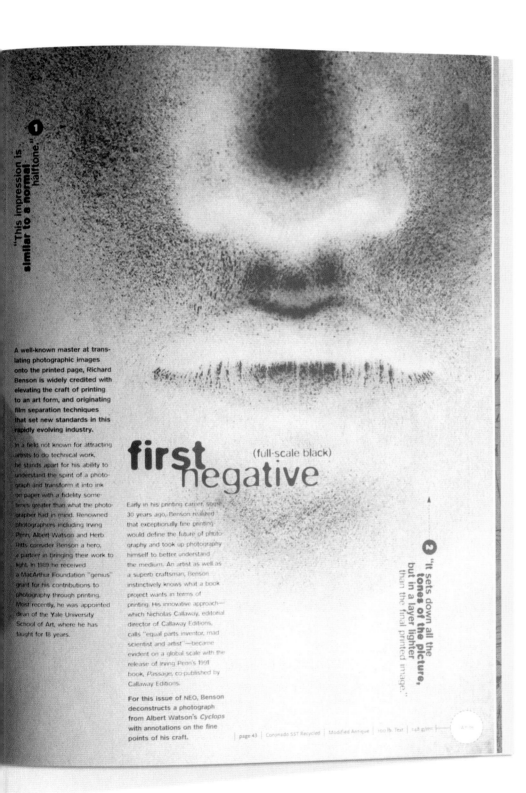

"This impression is similar to a normal halftone." ❶

A well-known master at translating photographic images onto the printed page, Richard Benson is widely credited with elevating the craft of printing to an art form, and originating film separation techniques that set new standards in this rapidly evolving industry.

In a field not known for attracting artists to do technical work, he stands apart for his ability to understand the spirit of a photograph and transform it into ink on paper with a fidelity sometimes greater than what the photographer had in mind. Renowned photographers including Irving Penn, Albert Watson and Herb Ritts consider Benson a hero, a partner in bringing their work to light. In 1989 he received a MacArthur Foundation "genius" grant for his contributions to photography through printing. Most recently, he was appointed dean of the Yale University School of Art, where he has taught for 18 years.

first
(full-scale black)
negative

Early in his printing career, some 30 years ago, Benson realized that exceptionally fine printing would define the future of photography and took up photography himself to better understand the medium. An artist as well as a superb craftsman, Benson instinctively knows what a book project wants in terms of printing. His innovative approach— which Nicholas Callaway, editorial director of Callaway Editions, calls "equal parts inventor, mad scientist and artist"—became evident on a global scale with the release of Irving Penn's 1991 book, *Passages*, co-published by Callaway Editions.

For this issue of NEO, Benson deconstructs a photograph from Albert Watson's *Cyclops* with annotations on the fine points of his craft.

❷ "It sets down all the tones of the picture, but in a layer lighter than the final printed image."

page 43 | Coronado SST Recycled | Modified Antique | 100 lb. Text | 148 g/m²

Given carte blanche to curate content, we identified new cultural trends, like the rise in local microbreweries. Unlimited production budgets let us fulfill long-held design fantasies to hire phenomenal artists like David Goldin to illustrate our beer story. With no limitations or excuses, the stakes were high to one-up the work of legendary designers, such as Woody Pirtle and Jim Cross, who had done previous issues of *NEO*. The experience inspired us to later design and publish our own books.

99 bottles of beer

What started Out in the Pacific Northwest as a grassroots movement against lackluster mass-marketed beers has turned into a national trend. Micro-breweries have proliferated in number more than thirty-fold over the past decade, and at brew pubs across the country, Americans are rediscovering the true taste of real beers. These micro-brews are often called "craft beers" because that aptly describes the personal craftsmanship that goes into each bottle. Produced in boutique operations that typically yield less than 15,000 barrels a year, microbreweries emphasize quality over volume. Only malt barley—and none of the cheaper corn and rice grains added by mass producers—goes into these micro-suds. And unlike national distributors that develop beers for the broadest consumer appeal, micro-brewers love to explore the many styles of malt barley beverages found around the world—pale ales, brown ales, German bocks, English bitters, Belgian fruit beers, lagers, stouts, porters, pilseners, barley-wine, wheat beers, and spiced winter brews. Made in small quantities to assure freshness and often preservative-free, most craft beers are sold regionally—sometimes just to customers who frequent the brew pub. Such freshness is essential to beer connoisseurs who explain that it helps to show off the complexity of flavors in well-crafted beers. Today, micro-brews command just 2 percent of the $40 billion American beer market, but consumption is growing by 50% annually. It's more than the distinctive taste of local brews that customers love. They are also drawn to the feeling of community created by neighborhood brew pubs and taverns. In graphic imagery, both for packaging and signage, microbreweries are reinforcing this hometown spirit by focusing on local nostalgia and traditions and the friendly familiarity that distinguishes them from distant national beer giants.

Navajo White | Sundance | Vellum | 80 lb. Text | 118 g/m² | **page 12**

New York, NY, 1999   Using dogs to sell invest-ments? Our client, the owner of the financial services firm Greystone, needed a brochure to explain his highly diversified, multi-dimensional company to potential investors. He's in a con-servative business but he loved our unexpected, off-the-wall design that plays up the shared qualities of Greystone and man's best friend. And he doesn't even own a dog.

A great client is one who is courageous, collaborative, and committed to quality. The CEO of Greystone embodied all three. This company offers a broad range of financial products and services. As with most similar firms, they are selling intangibles. When we asked the client to describe attributes that set his firm apart from their competitors, he quickly cited responsiveness, tenacity, resourcefulness, supportiveness, and strength as distinctive qualities.

Looking for an analogy that could provide a visual link to these characteristics, we suggested that illustrations of different breeds of dogs might do the trick. We got an instant green light to pursue this offbeat idea, starting with the cover.

Greystone lending programs include:

FHA Lending
(Multifamily properties, assisted living facilities
—Acquisitions
—Bridge financing
—Default workouts
—Equity financing
—New construction/substantial
—Refinancing

FannieMae DUS Lending
—Acquisition financing
—Bond credit enhancement

A
Different
Breed

GREYSTONE

Study One
**The Holtzman and
Silverman Companies
Ann Arbor, Michigan**

—$60 million property refinancing.
—Reduced interest expense dramatically.
—Closed in six weeks.

For the dog illustrations, we needed an artist who could strike the balance between capturing the essence of a breed and expressing particular character traits shared with Greystone. We chose to collaborate with Mark Ulriksen, whose covers for *The New Yorker* are always a great blend of sophistication and humor. We also loved Ulriksen's painterly style, which added warmth to what was essentially a serious technical brochure.

Timing is money. You can't win with just muscle. You need speed and agility— the power to seize an opportunity when it arises. So while Greystone has grown in size, we have stayed lean and hungry to respond quickly to our clients' needs— whether big or small. Our approach stems from our entrepreneurial spirit. It's a "challenge us" attitude combined with

Responsive

As a finishing touch, we worked with Frank Oswald, a great copywriter, to complement the images with a relaxed and confident editorial style.

Our novel approach was a bit risky for such a conservative business. However, our client saw it as a real plus. He said, "If someone doesn't get this point of view, they're probably not the right customer for us." The concept helped to filter the best business to Greystone.

Resourceful

Study Three
Finger Development Company
Houston, Texas

—$20 million bond refunding.
—Completed with minimal additional owner capital.
—Non-conventional financing structure.
—Resolved complex legal and tax-exempt bond issues.

"How in the world did they do that?"
Our competitors ask the question all
of the time. Greystone's extensive capital
markets experience and creative
approach to financing enable us to seize
opportunities that other companies find

Mexico City, Mexico, 2009 As members of the prestigious Alliance Graphique Internationale (AGI), Leslie and I were invited, along with 100 other designers, to celebrate Frida Kahlo and Diego Rivera in a poster to be displayed at an exhibition in Mexico City. There was no creative brief other than, "It's about Frida and Diego." For me, that meant I had to design a poster about art and love.

Creative freedom can be a double-edged sword. When the possibilities are too open-ended, the blank page can be threatening as well as thrilling. In the case of Kahlo and Rivera, I decided that their artistic marriage was one of equals, with each making their own contribution to the world of art, so the poster composition had to be symmetrical.

I began with portrait sketches of each of the artists from old photographs so I could "get to know them." I studied their art and read about their often fiery relationship. Finally, I chose the playing card composition, as they were both artistic royalty, and the suit of hearts because of their legendary romance. How you hang the poster depends on a personal preference for one artist over the other. It's a two-for-one solution.

Seattle, WA, 2000   The stunning photographs of the high-end stock agency <u>Corbis Images</u> needed little explanation. But combining images in a surprising way made designers take a second look.

There are millions of stock photographs available to designers at the click of a mouse, with more added every day. On one hand, this makes for a creative gold mine for projecting a wide range of emotions. But how does one stock photography agency stand apart from another? With Corbis Images, a company owned by Bill Gates, we decided that big and bold was the way to go. Our overscale brochure, *Hot Buttons*, presented provocative juxtapositions of images that made visual statements about contemporary cultural and societal issues.

We were given free rein to direct the editorial and decided to explore highly charged themes, such as obesity, media saturation, smoking, and world hunger. For example, contrasting a tight shot of sugary donuts with details of human navels created an interesting visual relationship, while the accompanying text was a commentary on America's penchant for unhealthy eating.

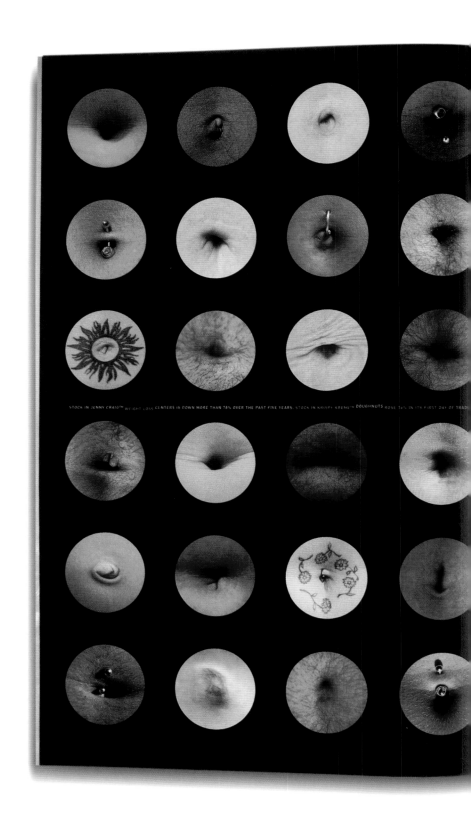

DIET VS. DOUGHNUTS

Another spread depicts a diagrammatic arrangement of multiple photographs, highlighting the inescapable bombardment of images in our daily lives. The result of this brochure was a memorable demonstration of the depth and quality of the Corbis Images library, and a reminder of the power of photography to communicate engaging messages.

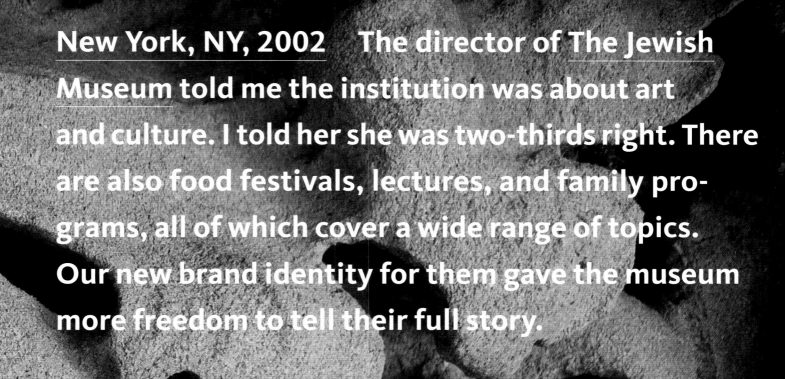

New York, NY, 2002   The director of The Jewish Museum told me the institution was about art and culture. I told her she was two-thirds right. There are also food festivals, lectures, and family programs, all of which cover a wide range of topics. Our new brand identity for them gave the museum more freedom to tell their full story.

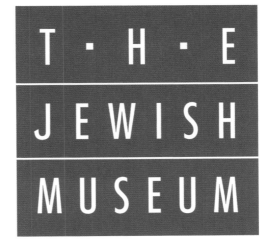

For over a century, The Jewish Museum has illuminated the Jewish experience, both secular and religious, demonstrating the strength of Jewish identity and culture. But it's also an inclusive institution with a very diverse membership. Housed in an imposing mansion on upper Fifth Avenue in Manhattan, the museum needed a fresh new identity that spoke to its contemporary and often provocative exhibitions. Our multi-colored logo and graphic program provided a liberating contrast to the staid image of the building, while making the museum more inviting to a broader audience.

The key to this program was the editorial signature composed of a flexible phrase that stated the mission of the museum as "Art & Culture," but then adding a third word depending on the specific event or artist they wanted to promote. For example, on an invitation to a dance performance, the signature would be "Art, Culture & Dance"; the branded title of the monthly members' publication became "Art, Culture & News"; and "Art, Culture & Discovery" headlined an informational brochure for museum visitors.

We developed a comprehensive set of brand-identity guidelines to be used by in-house designers and various agencies developing promotional materials for the museum. The overall freedom by which designers interpreted the identity continuously revitalized this esteemed institution.

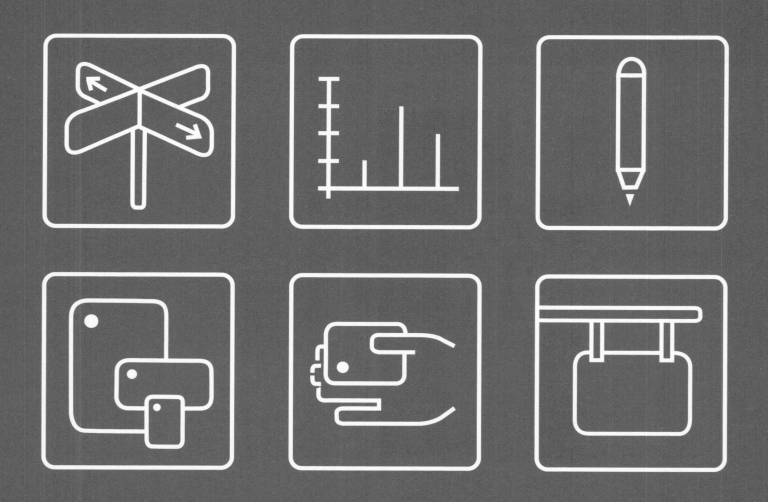

New York, NY, 2003   When we do pro-bono work, we will forego money for freedom, but under one condition: The client must play by our rules. When the AIGA asked us to design the installation of their annual "365" exhibition, they accepted this arrangement. We got the freedom we needed and they got free design. Our concept was summed up in one word: Red.

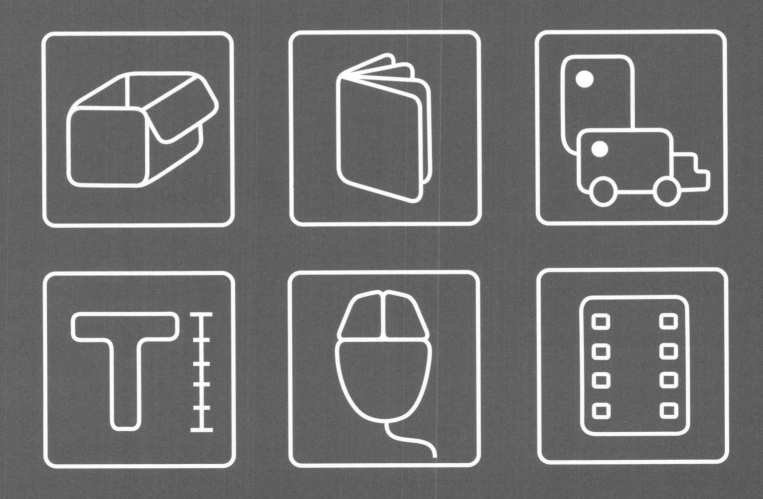

Twelve competitions, one show of excellence.

The Competitions

Each year, the AIGA, the professional association for design, exhibits the best work from a juried show of thousands of entries. It is quite a challenge to win, but an even greater challenge to design the winners' exhibition. The AIGA exhibit space is long and narrow, with high ceilings that can overwhelm the small scale of the graphic design entries.

We decided that the exhibit should be as exciting as the work itself. Painting the entire space bright red turned out to be surprisingly complementary to the posters, books, and brochures on view. We found durable floor tiles that could be customized in a brilliant shade of red and embedded with typography to complete the scheme. We also designed a pictogram for each of the juried categories as an additional graphic motif used on banners and promotions. It was a very bold move, but red is a color that designers love, and it electrified the feeling in the room.

Forward

"'It won't work.' 'We can't afford it.' 'People won't understand it.' My job is all about turning a 'no' into a 'yes.' Fortunately, I enjoy this." Ken

"I help companies build their brands. I help them communicate powerfully and effectively. I lead them where they need to go, whether they want to go there or not." Leslie

"I persevere. I don't give up. I have a lot of patience. And I make sure everything is perfect. If you have a great idea and you execute it poorly, then you've wasted a great idea." Leslie

"Because art and music have dominated my life, I lack some basic skills. Each year I try to add a new one to 'catch up.' A couple of years ago, I learned to swim. Next came touch-typing. Then learning to tie knots. However, I do know how to ride a bike." Ken

The Road to Success is Always Under Construction

Ken Carbone and Leslie Smolan have never stood still. They recognize that the one constant in the design business is change, and they make the most of an evolving world. "We take advantage of the opportunities that change offers," notes Leslie. "It has never been a threat to us."

That's good, because what designers do today is very different from what they did 35 years ago. "The profession has grown from a craft into something much more essential to business and society," says Ken. The very term "graphic design" was a suitable description of what he and Leslie did in 1977, but sounds limiting and outdated today. "When you consider that our work includes strategic planning, brand architecture, content development, video, music, websites, and apps, 'graphic design' just doesn't cut it anymore," suggests Ken. "And we're always debating whether the word 'branding' is a blessing or a curse," adds Leslie. The word helps their clients understand that they can amplify their message consistently across many applications, but it's become a ubiquitous term. Everyone from management consultants to public relations firms use it. And it can refer to everything from business strategy to celebrity endorsements.

The way design is viewed by the world at large has also been transformed dramatically—and for the better. "A few years ago, the trendy term 'design thinking' came into vogue, but we feel we've been practicing that for decades. We've always had both a right-brain and a left-brain perspective," says Leslie. "We're ecstatic that there is even a 'D' School at Stanford University. Design

2008
Taubman
We developed a brand identity
and marketing campaign for a leading
high-end retail mall operator.

2009
Mandarin Oriental Hotel Group
The website for The Residences at
Mandarin Oriental showcased their
properties around the world.

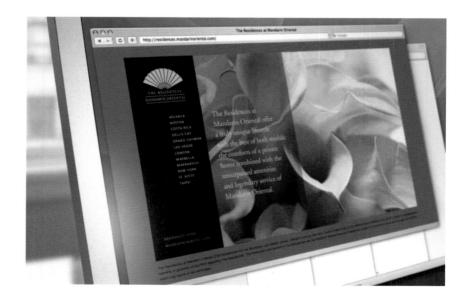

2010
Cravath, Swaine & Moore
We designed a website for this law firm by bringing the most relevant and current content to the forefront.

now has a seat at the big table," adds Ken. "We feel as if the best years for design, and the way we practice it, are ahead of us."

Technology is driving design into the mainstream. "More than ever, the world needs advocates who can provide experience and leadership on the intersection of content, technology, and design," says Leslie. She and Ken realize that technology is not just about gadgets: It's about new ways to communicate. They believe beauty in design is the artful integration of message and media, and today, they are more involved with drafting the story line than ever before. "Attention to detail and craft is essential in both words and pictures. Our best work happens when we can be in charge of both. And since the robots haven't taken over yet, it's humans who engage with what we do. So we want our work to be as evocative as possible," adds Leslie. "Whether our design inspires empathy, rage, amusement, or desire, emotions matter in communication."

As Ken puts it, "The technology world has a desperate need for us and what we do. A lot of the digital agencies approach things from an engineering mindset rather than from a design mindset," which means the functionality often takes precedence over the visual details. "We believe that to create a distinctive and memorable impression, you need both flawless functionality and beautiful design to enhance the way the

2010
Zest
Our concept for a new brand was
applied to prototype packaging for a
lemony soft drink.

2011
Canon U.S.A.
To inspire photographers, we created
"Idea Mine," our concept and design
for an iOS mobile application.

technology works. If you're going to push frontiers, it really helps to have some design basics under your belt," declares Leslie.

Carbone Smolan is doing both.

After 35 years, Ken and Leslie are careful about not resting on their laurels. "Success can be dangerous because it can take the edge off," maintains Ken. But three-and-a-half decades of experience means they can be selective about the work they undertake. "We don't want to be all things to all people. We want

2012
Regency Centers
A refreshed identity and advertising campaign gave a new voice to a national shopping center developer.

2012
SPE Certified
We developed an identity and website for a new food certification and consulting business that promotes healthy dining outside of the home.

2012
AIGA/NY
Ken contributed this whimsical poster
to celebrate the 30th anniversary
of the AIGA/NY.

to decide where we can have the most impact and work on projects that offer the greatest potential for creativity," explains Leslie. "And to work with people who 'get it,' because great clients lead to great design," adds Ken.

She and Ken won't be doing it alone. They are developing a new generation of leadership and talent at the agency. "The current crop of young designers is an exciting bunch," says Ken. "They're smart, articulate, and they bring a sense of pride and responsibility to their work, because they truly believe design can better the world."

Everyone involved understands the importance of maintaining the values and philosophies that Ken and Leslie have espoused since the beginning of their partnership: that playing it safe is no way to go through life, that their best work challenges what's possible, and that while it's great to win awards, at the end of the day the work has to work. But it's exploring new territory that's most exciting. "If we don't recognize the business five years from now, we'd consider that a resounding success," says Ken.

No matter how the future of design turns out, Ken and Leslie and their team will definitely have a hand in shaping it.

To be continued

"The best advice Leslie ever gave me?
'Don't date that woman—she's stupid.'
'Marry that woman—she's right for you.'" Ken

"Truth is essential. Even when it hurts." Leslie

Index

Acknowledgments:

With great appreciation and admiration, we thank Raul Barreneche for capturing us so eloquently in words. It took us 35 years to create this story, and mere months for him to write the synopsis. His enormous talent is overshadowed only by his personality, which made a potentially arduous process actually fun (and pain-free).

We extend a special thanks to design greats Massimo Vignelli and Steven Heller for generously contributing their thoughts and commentary on our work to this book.

Thank you to all the designers who had a hand in the creation of *"Dialog,"* beginning years ago with Amy Wang and Carla Miller, and ending with a herculean effort by Res Eichenberger, whose zen-like calm and laser-sharp eye for details transformed a massive pile of projects into a beautiful and coherent publication. We consider ourselves "Res-cued" by his care and dedication.

Without Suzanne Slesin and her team at Pointed Leaf Press, this book would still be a distant dream. Suzy brought her incredible skills as a writer, editor, and book maven to help bring order and clarity to our story, as well as frame our "world of design" for a wider audience. Her dynamic team of editors and producers—Deanna Kawitzky, Nyasha Gutsa, Regan Toews, and Marion D.S. Dreyfus—kept us in line and on schedule, not to mention grammatically correct. They in turn introduced us to Rino Varrasso and Zanardi Press in Italy, to ensure the book's exquisite reproduction. We also want to thank Beth Dickstein for introducing us to Pointed Leaf Press.

We would like to thank the following individuals, each of whom, in their own way, has been critical in shaping the Carbone Smolan Agency:

Marci Barbey, our CFO, has been with us for almost three decades. Marci brings precision, structure, and a no-nonsense approach that eludes many creative organizations. Her left-brain skills are complemented by her love of art, instilled by her father, a fine artist and portrait painter. Marci wears many hats at CSA, from finance director to legal advisor to head of human resources—she has handled tie break-ers, lectured us about bad habits, and provided us with an institutional memory. We would not be the same organization without her.

Carla Miller has been a design director at CSA for almost two decades, and has played a hand in many of the beautiful works on these pages. She has an exquisite sensitivity to type, color, and image, and can make even the simplest of design ingredients sing. Her design skills are complemented by an unerring command of print technology, resulting in work that is striking and subtly nuanced. She too comes from a family of designers, her father having been a long-time member of the in-house design team at IBM. Carla's attention to detail and finesse is evident throughout our work.

José Gomez has been our office manager for the past 12 years. He's a person who gets things done, whether that means organizing the work of others or just doing it himself. He keeps everything shipshape, from maintaining the workspace to organizing the archives, to feeding the studio at every Monday's staff meeting. He's our Rock of Gibraltar. We're extremely fortunate to have such a kind and honest person keeping the wheels of the machine running so smoothly.

Paul Pierson represents the future of this company. As a second-generation partner and design director, he's passionate about technology and design. Paul joined us in 2003 as an intern, and he's had an incredible trajectory since then, moving quickly through multiple positions and projects to emerge as a leader at the firm. He's intelligent and strategic, and enthusiastically mentors other designers to help them develop their talents and skills. Plus, he's an incredibly nice guy. In partnering with Paul and giving him the kinds of opportunities we had at such a young age, we are watching history repeat itself. In 2011, *Graphic Design USA Magazine* named him a "Person to Watch." We agree.

Special Thanks:

We are forever indebted to Fritz Gottschalk, who is, and has been, a mentor, collaborator, and most importantly, a life-long friend. From the very beginning, Fritz believed in us and did everything in his power to help us succeed. He taught us to think big, think global, and love white space. For that and so much more, we are eternally grateful.

And to the rest of our staff over the past 35 years:

Alyssa Adams
Anila Ago
Ernest Alfinez
Margaret Ames
Jodi Armstrong
Shannon Audino
Cynthia Auman
Craig Bailey
Lisa Bales
Beth Bangor
Melissa Barak
Marci Barbey
Mark Baskinger
J. Bauer
Gregor Beer
Karin Beutler-Fortin
Christa Bianchi
Wendy Blattner
S. Chadwick Blue
Carole Bouchard
Nicolle Boujaber-Diederichs
Jim Breazeale
Wendy Brennan
Erik Brokke
Katherine Bryan
Stacey Byrd
Bob Callahan
Susan Callahan
Tracey Cameron
Sue Carabetta
Diane Carbone
Sandi Carroll
Elizabeth Carstens
Hermes German Castaneda
Niña Cayaban
Catherine Cedillo (Abbenda)
Martine Channon
Lisette Cheresson
Midi Choe
Joey Cofone
Mary Anne Connolly
Amanda Copeland
Nora Cordero
Amelia Costigan
Molly Cottingham
Rachel Crawford
Anna Crider
Timea Dancs
Julie D'Andrea
Stacy Danon
David Decepida
Rosa Del Carmen
Donna Dempsey
Kim Dennis
Ruth Diener
Stacey Dietz
Ellyce DiPaola

Erika Doering
Jennifer Domer
Kristin Dudley
Melissa Duffner
Susan Dutton
Sterling Eason
Res Eichenberger
Joseph Eicher
Stephanie Eichman
Jennifer Escobar
Lee Ann Fahey
John Farrar
Ian Farrell
Lesley Feldman
Sarah Fels
Frances Fernandez
Caroline von Fluegge
Alison Franklin
Doug Freuh
George Ganginis
Jacob Gardner
Anita Genovese
Tyrone Gibson
David Goldstein
José Gomez
Catherine Goodman
Jenny Goodwyn
Cybele Grandjean
Melanie Green
Jennifer Greenstein
Erin Hall
Wendy Han
Richard Harris
Kyla Lange Hart
Jennifer Haynes
Dave Heasty
Stuart Henley
Karla Henrick
Kristine Hetzel
Lauren Hinson
Aaron Hitchcock
Shannon Holm
Ledra Horowitz
Wendy Hu
Bao-Tran Huynh
Laurie Hynes
Jung Hun Hyun
Moulsari Jain
Summer Jerue
Eun Joo Jun
Matt Juskiewicz
Nancy Kallile
Fritz Karch
Maynard Kaye
Andrea Kells
Shannon Kemper
Hasnain Khimji
Julie Kim
Karen Kizis

Christina Klumb
Denise Korn
Daniel Koval
Shannon Koy
Lesley Kunikis
Kristina Lamour
Jeanne La Pointe
Danielle La Senna
Melissa Laux
Caroline LaVopa
Aleana Leal
Jennifer Lee
Yvette Lenhart
Cynthia Levitt (Zaref)
Shawn Linder
Margaux Lushing
Gretchen Margetson
Patrina Marino
Andrew Marks
Nina Masuda
Tom Matt
Linda Matthews
Candy Mayo
Devrae McCants
Tim McCarthy
Melissa Menard
Andrew Miller
Carla Miller
Frederique Moinard
Lisa Mooney
Martina Muller
Mary Amy Mullins
Brendan Murphy
Brian Murphy
Kimiyo Nakatsui
Julie Nathon
Stephen Nebgen
Rosa Ng
John Nishimoto
Jane O'Connor
Nicole Ogg
Steve Orant
Lynn Paik
Judith Park
Prescott Perez-Fox
Holly (Sheila) Peters
Justin Peters
Paul Pierson
Eric Pike
Hiram Pines
Rebecca Pixley
Robin Plaskoff
Michael Plummer
Jayme Polin
Kamol Prateepmanowong
Eva Redette
Dominick Ricci
Angela Riddlespurger
Greg Rider

Ron Romero
Daryl Roske
Channing Ross
Michael Ross
Gayle Rutledge
Mariela Saito
George Sanchez
Fabian Schmid
Lisa Schneck
Bob Schroeder
Bob Seetin
Sam Seydel
Sheryl Shade
Samantha Shefts
Leslie Sherr
Laurel Shoemaker
Victor Sie
Rick Simner
Emily Singer
Andy Sir
Sharon Slaughter
Bryn Smith
Eric Smith
Hannah Smotrich
Adam Snetman
Tom Sopkovich
Robert Spica
Eric Spillman
Nick Spriggs
Jenny Staley
Allie Strauss
Vivien Sung
Jody Sutter
Greg Taube
Claire Taylor
Peter Taylor
Lionel Tepper
Jackie Thaw
Betsy Thomas
Jana Thompson
Miranda Thompson
David Uri
Isabella Von Buol Berenberg
Brock Waldron
Edna Walker
Peter Walker
Jeanne Walsh
Tristana Waltz
Amy Wang
Jonathon Warner
Rhonda Weiner
Susan Weingarten
Melanie Weisenthal
Elizabeth Weisman
Merja Welham
Stephanie Wenzel
Sherri Whitmarsh
Julie Wickware
Susan Wiengarten

Lorraine Wild
Allison Muench Williams
Jill Wittnebel
Ophelia Wong
Laura Wood
Samantha Woods
Ann Wukasch
Hideko Yamamoto

And to our mentors, friends, collaborators, and clients:

Hans Allemann
Ian Allen
Edna Andrade
Robin Andrews
Norma Arnold
Stuart Ash
Susan Ault
Laurence Bach
Cilla Bachop
Kim Baer
Barbara Barry
Nancy Batlin
Alan Becker
Lolly Becker
Moises Becker
Michael Begley
Jonathan Bell
Chad Bellisario
Harvey Bernstein
Émile Biasini
Lana Bilovus
Davide Bizzi
Kim Blanchette
Gene Blumberg
David Boorstin
Ramona Boston
Dan Boyarski
Peter Bradford
Betsy Bruce
Ken Burns
Carl Burton
Heather Bush
Alice Cahn
Chris Calori
Elsa Cameron
Arnold Carbone
James Carbone
Lucas Carbone
Nina Carbone
Robert Carlisle
Katherine Cartwright
A.M. Cassandre
Gene Castellano
Odile Chappelon
Ivan Chermayeff
Joyce Childress
Adriana Cisneros de Griffin
Mike Clifford

William Jefferson Clinton
Hillary Rodham Clinton
Janet Coombs
Susan Crandell
Michael Cronan
Bart Crosby
Jim Cummings
Kristen Cunningham
Grover Daniels
Tina Davis
Charles Day
Edgar Degas
Martina De Giorgis
Gregory Deligdisch
Keith De-Lin
Beth Dickstein
Jenny Dixon
Ben Dolmar
Sheila Donnelly
Shelley Dowell
Elad Dror
Inge Druckrey
Suzanne Duncan
Minerva Durham
Mary Durkin
Phillip G. Edwards
Anna Egger-Schlesinger
Jane Englebardt
Adelina Wong Ettelson
Don Fangmeyer
Deborah Brightman Farone
Sally Feldman
Jeff Franchetti
Rich Franconeri
Stephen Frandsen
Doris Freedman
Patrick Freeman
Gregory Furman
Michael Gallary
Tom Geismar
Steff Geissbuhler
Joanne Gerstel
Ira Glick
Keith Godard
Laurence Goldberg
Cliff Goldman
Fritz Gottschalk
Edith Graves
Bill Green
Steven Greenes
Richard Grefé
April Greiman
Adam Greiss
Susan Griffin
Claire Gruppo
Chris Hacker
David Halperin
Lucille Harasti
Hugh Hardy

Mark Harmon
Sylvia Harris
Steven Heller
Kenneth Hiebert
Armin Hoffman
Mary Holt
Malcolm Holzman
Emily Hopp
Michael Horst
Holly Hotchner
Anthony Iovino
Robert Ivy
Don Jaclin
Rita Jacobs
Lisa Jenks
Craig Jennings
Steve Jobs
Bruce Johnson
Judy Kalvin
Whitney Butler Kantor
Rachel Kash
James Kasschau
Steve Kaufman
Jamie Kennard
Curtis King
Stephanie Klein
Jill Kluge
Bryan Knapp
Jonathan Knowles
Susy Korb
Robert Krasnow
Barbara Kuhr
Michel Laclotte
Rick Landers
Noah Landow
Jacques Lamarre
Lawrence Lasser
Albert Lee
Forrest D. Leighton
Arthur Levitt
Renate Lindler
Caroline MacDonald
Karen MacDonald
Cheryl MacLachlan
William Mandel
Fred Martens
Frank Martinez
Ilse Mast-Gottschalk
David McFadden
Vince Meilus
Oscar Mertz
Muffie Meyer
Katherine Milton
Thelonius Monk
Kristen Moore
Dave Mowers
Brier G. Muse
Brian Napack
Christoph Oberli

Kathy O'Donnell
Caroline Ollivier
Beverly Ornstein
Frank J. Oswald
Graeme Outerbridge
Didi Pei
I.M. Pei
Sandi Pei
Shel Perkins
Carole Perry
Philippe Petit
William Phelan
Ave Pildas
François Pinault
Jane G. Pisano
Michael Plummer
John Plunkett
Stephen Pollan
Phillippa Polskin
Mike Racz
Paul Rand
Grace Rapkin
Mary Rawlinson
Peter Rea
Alex Reid
Hank Richardson
Peggy Roalf
Ana Rojas-Filliben
Michelle Rosen
Joan Rosenbaum
Steve Rosenberg
Jaron Rubenstein
Scott Rubenstein
Kristen Ruble
Thomas O. Ryder
Arthur Sachs
Laurie Salmore
Alec Sash
Bob Schaffer
Howard Schatz
Mike Scheiner
Anne Scher
Fran Schreiber
Martha Shapiro
William Shiebler
Laura Shore
Elaine Shusterman
Erika Silverstein
Alfred Sisto
Jean Sisto
Joanne Sisto
Brian Smith
Erik Smith
Jonah Smith
Rodney Smith
Savannah Smith
Gloria Smolan
Marvin Smolan
Rick Smolan

Sandy Smolan
Seth Smoot
Betty Snyder
James Snyder
Joy Solomon
Nil Sönmez
Steven Spiess
Carol Sprague
Bill Stein
Martin E. "Hap" Stein
Peter Steiner
Leslie Stoker
Frank Stork
Nancy Straetmans
Nan A. Talese
Chris Tardio
Robert Taubman
William Taubman
Tiit Telmet
Walter Thomas
Linda Tischler
Peter Tvarkunas
Dave Vanden-Eynden
David Van de Water
Emmanuel Verstraeten
Massimo Vignelli
Bart Voorsanger
Gina Elizabeth Vriens
Adam Wahler
Robyn Waters
Don Webb
Palmer West
Sherrie Westin
Yann Weymouth
Alina Wheeler
Marissa Wilcox
Michael Wilson
Karen Wise
Adam Witter
Cynthia Wornham
Walter Wriston
Jana Zednickova
Christa Zelinsky
Judith Zuk

Photography & Illustration Credits

All images were provided by the Carbone Smolan Agency. With the exception of the following list, projects were photographed by Cliff Doerzbacher and Gabriel Rinaldi. Every effort has been made to locate the copyright holders; any omissions or errors will be corrected in future printings.

Aether Apparel, 74
Quentin Bacon, 32–37
Kim Baer, 267
Tom Bonner, 118–121
Carnegie Fabrics, 110
Chicago Symphony Orchestra, 174
Lane Coder/Gallery Stock, 71
Corbis Images, 240–242
Philipe De Potestad, 59–63
T. Charles Erickson/Photograph from the Hartford Stage Production of "Noises Off," 146-147
Terry Ferrante, 10-11
Scott Frances/Otto Archive, 64-65
Andi Frank/Gallery Stock, 68-69
Erica Freudenstein, 188–191
Shannon Holm, 96
ICF Group, 138-139
David Levinthal, 180-181
Kit Morris/photoproducersf.com, 143
Natural History Museum of Los Angeles County, 112-113
Michael Parmelee, 108-109
John Prettyman/Panaro & Prettyman Photography, 98-99, 102
Howard Schatz, 164-165
Rodney Smith, 150-151, 159–160, 204-205
Seth Smoot, 176-177
John Still, 48-49
Tetra Images/Getty Images, 46
Mark Ulriksen/illustrations, 228-229
Eric Van Den Brulle/The Image Bank, Getty Images, 52-53
Veer, 84-85, 130
Paul Warchol, 80–83, 250
Albert Watson, "Golden Boy, New York City, 1990," 220-221

Project Credits

Carnegie Fabrics
    Digital rendering: Farm
Morgan Stanley
    Sign structure: Poulin + Morris Inc.
Nizuc
    Renderings: ARCHPARTNERS
The Jewish Museum
    Brochure and newsletter design: Eng & Yee Designs, Inc.
W.L. Gore & Associates
    Fabrication and installation: Showman Fabricators
    Facility renovation architect: Homsey Architects
W New York/Downtown
    Interiors: GRAFT
    W logo design: Mimi Sternlicht
    Renderings: ARCHPARTNERS